Variations on a Theme

Variations on a Theme

Alan Maley
Alan Duff

Cambridge University Press

Cambridge
London · New York · Melbourne

Published by the Syndics of the Cambridge University Press
The Pitt Building, Trumpington Street, Cambridge CB2 1RP
Bentley House, 200 Euston Road, London NW1 2DB
32 East 57th Street, New York, NY 10022, USA
296 Beaconsfield Parade, Middle Park, Melbourne 3206, Australia

First published 1978

Printed in Great Britain by
Richard Clay (The Chaucer Press), Ltd,
Bungay, Suffolk

ISBN 0 521 22059 9

Contents

Preface

Most published materials for listening comprehension focus on linguistic content. In contrast to this approach, the materials in this book place the main emphasis on the total context in which verbal interaction occurs.

The dialogues are relatively simple to understand as far as their content of vocabulary and structures is concerned. The listener is thus freed to concern himself with questions of meaning and intention: who is speaking to whom? where? in what circumstances? and why? It is these matters which are crucial for real comprehension, and yet have been thus far neglected.

The dialogues are grouped in sets of three or four, around a common theme (e.g. people waiting for something) and a common language function (e.g. asking whether it is necessary to do something or not). Almost all the dialogues are in some way mysterious or enigmatic, since it is rarely possible to say with certainty who or what is being talked about. This gives students a strong motivation for discussion. Indeed, the problem-solving aspect is one of the most original features of the material.

The language work exercises draw attention to the variety of ways in which an identical message can be expressed. For those who wish to go further, there are production exercises of a more creative kind, including written work, wherever this fits in naturally with the theme of the dialogues.

The aim throughout has been to provide interesting and entertaining material which can be used flexibly to suit different teaching situations. It should be regarded as a bank of resources to be drawn on whenever necessary.

A.M.
A.D.

Introduction

It often happens, during an average working day, that we find ourselves coming in on conversations which do not directly involve or concern us. These may be simple exchanges of greetings – between neighbours in the lift, shop-keeper and customer, colleagues at work – or they may be more structured conversations, such as arguments in the home, discussions on the telephone, instructions at work, etc. Even if we are not immediately involved, we can in most cases tell what has already been said (and predict what is likely to be said) from basic signals, such as tone of voice, length of pauses, gesture, or choice of words; these are some of the clues to what the speakers are *really* trying to tell each other. In our own language, we pick up these signals almost without thinking; in a foreign tongue, it is more difficult.

In *Variations on a theme*, it is above all *this* skill that we should like to develop: the ability to interpret fragments of speech, to listen for clues in what is said, and develop sensitivity to what is *not* said. For, it seems to us, many dialogues produced specifically for language learning sound 'unreal' not because the language itself is at fault but because too much is being said. If you listen closely to normal speech in your own language you will be struck by how little reference is made to *what* one is talking about, since this is often known to both speakers. This is not to say that we never refer to the topic, but that we do not usually comment on what is self-evident. To take a simple example, you may indeed say to someone: 'His hat is on the chair', but we are *least* likely to say it if the other person knows this. We would simply point, or say 'It's over there.' If, however, we had walked into a room looking for someone, it would have been reasonable to say 'His hat is on the chair', since this would have indicated that the missing person was somewhere in the building.

There seems to be little point, then, in using the dialogue form for teaching the spoken language unless it corresponds as closely as possible to the *way* in which we speak and not just to the words we use. Saying and meaning are not the same: the same form of words can mean different things in different circumstances. What is said may not be meant, and what is meant may not be said. In these dialogues, therefore, we have tried not to be unnecessarily explicit. Our aim is to imagine that we have broken in on other people's conversations and that we are interested in finding out what they have been talking about or are still discussing. And, to make this 'detective work' more rewarding, we offer in each set of dialogues a number of alternative ways of expressing the same function. Here is an example, in which the key function is *expressing surprise*:

1   A: *They've found it!*
    B: *No! Where?*
    A: *On top of a six-storey building.*
    B: *Impossible!*

2   A: *We know where it is!*
    B: *Do you?*
    A: *Aren't you pleased?*
    B: *Oh, yes ... Well, where is it?*
    A: *Just across the street – on the top floor of that building.*
    B: *That's odd.*
    A: *Why?*
    B: *Because I found it yesterday – in the cellar!*

3   A: *It's turned up at last.*
    B: *Yes, I know.*
    A: *You know!?*
    B: *Yes, it's on top of Broadcasting House.*
    A: *But you can't possibly have known. Unless....*
    B: *Unless ...?*

Here we are just as interested in what is *not* said as in what is. We do not know who A and B are, nor do we know what the mysterious 'it' is. But there are indications in the dialogues, which, if we follow them up, will enable us to suggest possible interpretations – our *own* interpretations.

As you will notice, the characters in these dialogues have no names. This is partly because we wished to avoid 'identifying' them, and partly because people do not, in fact, refer to one another by name as often as text-books would have us think. In order to apologise, Mr Brown and Gary Glitter may both in fact use the same language ('I'm sorry ...'), but if their names were to appear in the margin, the words would immediately assume the personality of the speaker, and the dialogue would no longer be open-ended.

It is by choice that we have left the dialogues open-ended, because our aim was that they should be used for *discussion* and *interpretation* rather than imitation and reproduction. They are designed to give a sample of what might be *heard* in the language, *not* necessarily of what one might be expected to produce. The question of production will be considered in the section 'How to use the variations'.

Another of our aims was to offer a range of expression in the spoken language. This is why the dialogues are called *Variations on a theme*. As we all know from our own language, the same thing may be said in many different ways, according to our mood, intention, relation to the other speaker, and so on. As native speakers, we often hit instinctively on the best way of expressing ourselves. We know, too, when we may interrupt, when we may leave a sentence unfinished, and when we need to clarify ourselves. We listen to others, and adapt our speech to what they say. In the foreign tongue our range is necessarily more restricted. This, however, is no reason why we should not fully appreciate and understand the language used by a native speaker, even if we might find it hard or even impossible to imitate. Through intelligent listening, too, we may hope gradually to assimilate some of what we hear into our own speech. This is why we have decided to give the texts of the dialogues, in the hope that the students will use the speakers' words to back up their arguments in the discussion rather than parrot them in class repetition exercises.

What are the variations?

For the sake of convenience, one important function has been highlighted in each set of dialogues (a *function* being an operation commonly performed in any language, such as *agreeing* or *disagreeing, accepting* or *rejecting* an offer, etc.). Each function is illustrated in three or four ways, and these are the *variations*. For example, under the function of *apologising*, the following expressions – which might be said to transmit the function – occur in the dialogues:

I've come to apologise . . .
Sorry, if I woke you last night.
Please excuse me for disturbing you.
I'd like to apologise . . .
Oh, I'm extremely sorry.
O.K., I'm sorry.

Clearly, it is not necessary for the student to be able to handle actively the entire range of expressions involved in any one function. He should, nevertheless, be able to understand and interpret them. Naturally, although only one function has been selected for detailed treatment, each set of dialogues inevitably contains other functions. It is only for convenience that one has been singled out.

The description of the functions was inspired by the list drawn up by the Council of Europe for *The Threshold Level* and we have used their headings for the different sections.* We have, however, made our own deletions and additions. It would have been impossible to work out all the functions exhaustively. We have tried, however, to select those which appear to be most commonly used, and to illustrate the language most frequently connected with each. A word on this point to language teachers in particular: you will certainly be struck by the fact that material based on functional lines does not follow the structural and grammatical grouping usually imposed by text-books. The above example, for instance, includes a present tense, a present perfect (in form only), two conditional forms, and a 'polite' imperative! Do not feel that this is suddenly too much for you to handle. The dialogues, you will find, have been kept as short as possible and the load of new lexical items is very light. Occasionally, as in unit 2.4, you may strike a word (e.g. 'warped'), which will need explaining before the students listen to the dialogues, but on the whole they should have no trouble with vocabulary. Remember, too, that the student is not necessarily being required to repeat what he hears. These are certainly not dialogues-for-learning-by-heart!

Level

This brings us to the question of level. Although the vocabulary required is relatively restricted, the student working with these dialogues would be expected to have a grasp of all the essential structures of the language. In fact, the so-called 'complex structures' (past conditional, passive using the continuous form, etc.) appear relatively infrequently, since the material was not conceived for the teaching of structures. This means that here, too, the student should have no difficulty in recognising the forms used. Where his problem may arise is in the idiomatic meaning of what is, to him, a familiar structure ('Well I was just wondering . . .' or 'I still seem to remember'). If this is a problem, however, it is one worth facing up to. We have taken care to ensure that the language represents *commo*

* See: *The Threshold Level*, by J. A. Van Ek, L. G. Alexander, J. L. M. Trim *et al.*, Council of Europe, 1975.

rather than *rare* usage, which means that structures used idiomatically will often be self-explanatory in context. It should also not be forgotten that the students will first *hear* the dialogues and that they will initially be reacting to the spoken word.

Who could use the *variations*, then? We feel that they would appeal to adult learners with a 'school' knowledge of English interested in going further with it for some practical purpose. They could also be used by secondary school students in their last two years of learning.

How to use the book

As we have said earlier, these dialogues are intended essentially for *interpretation* and *discussion*. The reason we have not placed great emphasis on imitation and reproduction is that, from experience, we have discovered that students – with certain exceptions – do not easily assume a ready-made role. When the words are not theirs, they become awkward. If, instead of being required to reproduce the words (which have anyway lost their freshness by being fixed), they are able to talk *about* what has been said and to mould this into their own speech by referring back to the original, they will unconsciously reproduce those parts of the dialogue that are necessary for discussion, e.g. 'He wouldn't have said "I beg your pardon" if he had been talking to his sister!'

Although it is not necessary for students to listen to *all* the dialogues before moving on to discussion, we believe it is essential that the initial listening be done without looking at the texts. This is to ensure that the students first discuss what they have *heard*, basing their interpretation on the spoken rather than the written word. The functional framework is not stressed, because we want the student to concentrate on what he hears and understands, not on a particular function or structure.

After each set of dialogues there is an *interpretation* exercise. On the whole, the pattern of questioning does not vary greatly from set to set. Nevertheless, in some dialogues it is easier to decide who is involved than in others. We have tried to bear this in mind. The questions suggested under *interpretation* should be borne in mind while listening, even though they may not be answered until later in group discussion.

Each set of dialogues is also followed by *some useful ways of expressing the function*. These suggestions should be used when students engage in the production exercises involving parallel situations or extending the given dialogues. Clearly the choice of one rather than another way of expressing a given function will depend upon the contextual feature (role, status etc.) which will have been dealt with during the listening and discussion phase. Every opportunity should be taken for discussing the reasons for choosing a given language form in a specific context.

The *production* exercises should be done only if time permits; they may be done independently, in a later class, if necessary. In these exercises, we have tried to find ways of getting the listener himself to use the language – not necessarily that of the dialogues – which is related to the function in question. For this reason a number of games and expansion exercises have been introduced: these offer the opportunity to move away from the constraints of the dialogue towards a freer and more individual use of the language. *Written* exercises have been introduced only where they seemed to stem naturally from the dialogue material.

The Appendix at the back is supplementary material intended mainly for use by the teacher. The *possible interpretations* are in no way 'solutions'; they are ideas which the students might like to consider once they have arrived at their own conclusions. There is no single 'correct' interpretation for any of the dialogues and we have deliberately given our own suggestions in an order which does not follow that of the dialogues, so as to dissuade the student from merely turning to the suggestions and expanding them. We hope that people using the book will have sufficient confidence in their own interpretations not to be tempted to search for a 'right answer'. In these exercises, everyone has a right to his own opinion, as long as he is prepared to justify it to his colleagues.

Before using the dialogues, please remember that this is *not* a course book and that it does not offer a graded study programme. It is material to be used in conjunction with course work, and so we suggest that you do not try more than one or two sets of dialogues at a time. We also suggest that, as the units are not arranged in a graded sequence, you should feel free to use them in any order which is convenient. They should certainly not be worked through exhaustively from beginning to end.

Practical suggestions

Although several dialogues are presented in each unit, experience has shown that students cannot cope with more than one at a time. We therefore suggest you try any of the following strategies, although in our experience the first has proved to be the most effective.

A Choose one dialogue to concentrate on.
   i) Play it once, without any introduction or any instructions, other than to listen carefully.
   ii) After the students have listened, there are certain general questions you might ask (and these are common to any of the dialogues), e.g.

   How many speakers/people are involved?
   How old are they?
   Are they strangers/close friends? Do they seem to like each other? Does it matter?
   Can you tell where they might be: *inside* – a small, private/large, public room; *outside* – in the country/a city/a street/etc.?
   Have you any idea what they might be talking about?
   Did any single word strike you as being important? (e.g. was it repeated?)
   Can you remember any phrases from the dialogue?

   These will only be immediate impressions. The class should be asked simply to offer their suggestions, but not to elaborate on them. Discussion is undesirable at this stage because it will inhibit fuller exchange of opinion in groups later on.
   iii) Now divide the class into groups (of three to five per group). Tell them that the dialogue will be played twice more and that they should listen to decide whether their first impressions are justified.
   Allow a maximum of ten minutes for this.
   There are now two possible ways of continuing:
   a) each group nominates a spokesman to give its version of the facts to the whole class,
   b) alternatively, stage a) can be omitted and you pass straight on to a further playing of the dialogue. This time, the groups will be able to follow the text and will be looking for the answers to the questions in the book. When answers have been found, each group sends a spokesman to another group to present and defend his own group's solutions.
   Another worthwhile way of rounding off this part of the activity (especially if groups cannot agree on any one solution) is to ask each student individually to write out his own explanation as briefly as possible. Students may then

exchange their written versions, and, if they wish, discuss them orally.

iv) Play the same dialogue again. This time ask the students (who will have the text before them) to note the phrases or sentences which express the key function, e.g. in *Asking about agreement or disagreement*

Don't you think?
Don't you agree?
Really?
I think . . . don't you? etc.

Ask the students if they can think of other ways of expressing the same function. Some ideas are given after the exercises accompanying each set of dialogues, but these are by no means exhaustive.

v) You can now proceed with the *production* and, where relevant, the *writing* exercises.

B   Follow the instructions for A i, ii, iii, but do this for *all* the dialogues in the unit. (This is a strategy which requires much more time than is usually available.)
   You would then move on to A iv, i.e. a comparison of the exponents of the key function in each of the dialogues.

C   A somewhat different approach to the dialogues is the following in which the emphasis is on the situational elements rather than the variations in the expression of the key function.
   In this case, you follow steps i and ii of A for *each* of the dialogues in the unit. Discussion then centres on what distinguishes the situation in each of the dialogues from the others.

The *production* exercises vary, but the general pattern is to move from extension of the dialogues to personal adaptation of the idea (or function). Clearly, it is up to you to introduce any ideas of your own at this point. For some of the production exercises certain materials may be needed, e.g. pictures. Before trying out the exercises, be certain that you have what you need.

In *writing*, which often overlaps with *production*, we have tried to give exercises in which it would be meaningful to write. For example, in the unit on *stating logical conclusions* 'Imagine you are the person A and B were waiting for. You do not meet them. Write a note in which you explain why you were late; apologise or blame, depending on whose fault it was that you were late.' As far as possible, the written exercises serve a purpose which is not merely that of description. What the students put down on paper is meant to be *read*, and it is therefore important that they should actually read each other's writing.

Make sure that enough time is left at the end for the recording to be played once again. The students will then have the opportunity of hearing the dialogues with their own interpretations in mind. At this stage, but *not* before, they might like to compare their own interpretations with those given as suggestions in the Appendix.

In conclusion, we recommend that you treat the *variations* rather like medicine – to be taken in small doses only! Although we have deliberately not stressed the possibilities of dramatisation and performance, these should not be precluded. The dialogues are, on the whole, very sparse. If the students are interested, they should be encouraged to flesh them out and present their own versions to each other, preferably as pair to pair rather than group to group.

We hope you will find the material helpful in linking two skills that are too often kept apart – listening comprehension and oral production.

Part one:
Imparting and seeking factual information

1.1 That's him
(Identifying)

1 A: *Hey, that's him, isn't it?*
  B: *Hm? Where?*
  A: *Down there. In brown . . .*
  B: *But it can't be!*
  A: *That's what I thought. But he's got exactly the same . . .*
  B: *Wait, I'll try and get closer . . .*

2 A: *Well, I suppose that must be him.*
  B: *I suppose so.*
  A: *Not quite what I expected . . .*
  B: *No . . . not really. Perhaps . . .*
  A: *Hold it . . . Yes, yes it's him all right. Remember they said . . .*

3 A: *There he is.*
  B: *Where?*
  A: *Over there. He's over there. Look.*
  B: *Him!*
  A: *No, the other one. In the fawn-coloured coat.*
  B: *Oh, that's him!*

4 A: *Right. He's here.*
  B: *Where?*
  A: *Outside.*
  B: *Which one?*
  A: *You'll see. He's wearing brown.*
  B: *Anything else?*
  A: *No . . . But when he looks at you, he looks like this . . .*

Interpretation

Try to identify A and B in each case.
What connection is there between them?
Who is the person they are talking about?
Where do you think these dialogues take place?
What are A and B doing? Walking? Standing? Waiting?
Why are they looking at the man in brown?
Is the man in brown aware of them?
What do you think A and B were doing before the dialogues began?
What will happen next?

Some useful ways of identifying

It's a . . ./That's a . . .   There's a . . .
It's . . ./They're . . .   That's it!
He's . . .   That's him!
He's got a . . .   There it is.
She has a . . .   There he is.

Production

Divide into groups of eight or ten. Each group should stand in a circle, and everyone should look carefully at everyone else. After a few minutes, everyone should close their eyes. One person should leave the room. The circle must now decide who is missing and what he or she was wearing.

This can then be repeated once or twice, with several people leaving the room at a time and exchanging articles of clothing, jewellery, etc. When they return, the others in the circle must try to spot the changes.

1.2 No, not like that
(Correcting)

1 A: *Left.*
   B: *No, right.*
   A: *I don't want to argue, but . . .*
   B: *Don't you remember that stone?*
   A: *And it was after the stone!*
   B: *It wasn't, you know.*
   A: *All right, if you say so . . .*

2 A: *I think you've just passed it, actually . . .*
   B: *No, it's still some way from here.*
   A: *Oh, I see . . . It's just that I seem to remember that stone . . .*
   B: *Yes . . . ?*
   A: *And I thought it was just after that . . .*
   B: *No, it's the next one, in fact.*

3 A: *There we are. That's it . . .*
   B: *Ah–hah.*
   C: *No, you've got the wrong one!*
   A: *How do you mean?*
   C: *Well, isn't that where the big stone thing was?*
   A: *No, you've got them mixed up. That was the next one . . . Now, here we are . . .*

4 A: *No, they didn't!*
   B: *Are you sure?*
   A: *They said* not *the one after the stone.*
   B: *Before the stone, you mean.*
   A: *No, after . . .*

Interpretation

Who do you think A and B are? Who is C in dialogue 3?
What age might they be?
Do they know each other well?
Where do you think A and B are?
What are they trying to find? Or what are they trying to do?
In each dialogue there is some kind of disagreement. What is this about?
Who do you think 'they' are in dialogue 4?

Some useful ways of correcting

Yes, but . . .
No, it wasn't.
No, that's not right/true/correct.
That's wrong.
Not exactly . . .
and declarative sentences containing negation words such as nothing, never, nobody, no, etc.

Production

A picture will be needed for each person in the class. Divide into groups of five. Each group should take five pictures and examine them together, looking for detail. After about five minutes, the pictures should be turned face downwards. Each person should take one, which he shows to no-one else.

Now, in turn, each member of the group should get the others to try and reconstruct his picture. The person who is holding the picture should let the group discuss the details as much as possible before giving them the 'right' answer. Members of the group should correct one another.

1.3 Are you sure?
(Checking up)

1 A: . . . when did you say?
   B: *Fifteen thirty.*
   A: *I see . . .*
   B: *Anything else?*
   A: *Well, I was just wondering . . . There isn't an earlier one, is there?*
   B: *No, nothing before three thirty.*
   A: *Nothing? . . . Right. Thank you.*

2 A: *Where are you going?*
   B: *It's time already.*
   A: *Nonsense. You've got another three hours.*
   B: *Are you sure?*
   A: *Absolutely.*
   B: *'Cos I wouldn't like it to be like last time, you know.*

3 A: *Did you say this morning?*
   B: *Yes. Why?*
   A: *Oh . . . it's just that I thought it was this afternoon.*
   B: *No. Not as far as I know . . .*
   A: *Right. Then I'll make the arrangements.*
   B: *Good.*
   A: *Would you mind if I just made quite sure?*

4 A: *Oh, 'bout three thirty.*
   B: *Not before?*
   A: *Aw . . . doubt it.*
   B: *You're quite sure, are you?*
   A: *Well, it might be later of course . . .*

Interpretation

Suggest who A and B might be in each dialogue. How are they related? Are they friends? Do they work together? Have they just met?

Where are A and B?

How long have they been there?

What do you think A is asking about?

Why does A question B's replies?

Before dialogues 1 and 3 begin, what do you think B has just said to A? What will happen at the end of these dialogues.?

Some useful ways of checking-up

Is it?

Is there?

Is she?

Are they? etc.

and all question-tag forms (isn't it? don't you? will it? etc.)

Are you sure?

Are you quite certain?

Production

Pictures containing a fair amount of detail will be needed. Divide into pairs. Each pair should take a picture, examine it for about five minutes, then exchange pictures with another pair. The two pairs should now question each other concerning the content of their pictures. The examining pair should try to avoid blunt negative responses (like 'No, it isn't') to the other pair's suggestions, and encourage the other pair to think again by using phrases such as 'Are you sure?', 'You think it was *red*, do you?'

1.4 Could you tell me . . . ?
(Asking)

1 A: *He's not in, I'm afraid.*
   B: *Yes, but could you tell me when he'll be back?*
   A: *I'm sorry, I don't know.*
   B: *Well, do you think I could leave a message for him?*
   A: *If you like . . .*

2 A: *He'll be back in a moment. Won't you come in?*
   B: *No thank you. I can't wait. Do you know when he's expected?*
   A: *I'm sure he won't be long.*
   B: *Yes . . . yes. Would you mind taking a message for him?*
   A: *Not at all, only I'm leaving in five minutes, you see.*

3 A: *Phil?*
   B: *No, Doris.*
   A: *Oh, I'm sorry . . . Is Phil in, do you know?*
   B: *Yes, I do. No, he isn't.*
   A: *I see. When's he coming back then?*
   B: *No idea.*
   A: *Mind if I leave a message?*
   B: *Suit yourself.*

4 A: *No . . . no . . . Haven't seen him for ages.*
   B: *I see. And you've no idea when he'll be back?*
   A: *No, none at all.*
   B: *In that case, I'd like to leave a note. May I?*
   A: *Oh, of course. Go right ahead.*

5 A: *Well, where is she?*
   B: *I can't tell you.*
   A: *You mean you won't!*
   B: *I mean I can't!*
   A: *Well, perhaps you'll be kind enough to give her a message!*
   B: *What makes you think I'll see her?*

Interpretation

Who are A and B in each dialogue? How old are they? How well do they know each other?

Are there any dialogues in which you think one of the speakers is being rude? Telling a lie? Embarrassed? Deliberately being unhelpful?

Who do you think A wants to see in each case? What is B's relation to that person?

Some useful ways of asking

All typical question forms, including WH–questions and HOW . . .
Can . . . ?
Could . . . ?
Do (you mind if) . . . ?

Have . . . ?
Is . . . ?
Would (it/he) . . . ?
Is it all right if . . . ?
Do you think I could?

Production

Choose two of the dialogues and decide why A wants to leave a message in each case. Now write the message. Remember that it is being written to a third person (C). Make it clear, through your choice of language, what the relation is between A and C. This should not take more than ten minutes. When you have finished, exchange notes or messages with others in the class and try to work out which dialogues their notes refer to.

1.5 Anyone happen to know?
(Asking)

1 A: *D'you know what time it is?*
   B: *No idea.*
   A: *Eleven!*
   B: *Eleven? It can't be! . . . Oh, of course, I forgot.*

2 A: *. . . well, I wonder what time it is . . .*
   B: *Oh, it must be getting on for eleven, I'd say.*
   A: *Eleven! Already!*
   B: *I had no idea it was so late . . .*
   A: *Yes, I'm afraid I'll really have to . . .*
   B: *Well, it's a pity, but I don't want to keep you . . .*

3 A: *Excuse me, do you happen to have the time?*
   B: *I make it . . . uh . . . just coming up for eleven.*
   A: *Eleven?*
   B: *Uh . . . yes . . . yes . . . just coming up for eleven.*
   A: *Are you sure?*
   B: *Well, I mean . . . er . . .*

4 A: *Do you realise what time it is?*
   B: *Oh, 'bout eleven . . .*
   A: *Well?*
   B: *Well. It's not all that late.*

5 A: *Hey, what's the time?*
   B: *Eleven.*
   A: *Hell!*
   B: *Too late?*
   A: *Too late.*

6 A: *Anybody got the time?*
   B: *Eleven – on the dot.*
   A: *Right. Are we ready then?*
   B: *Ready!*

Interpretation

Suggest who A and B might be in each dialogue.

Pick out those dialogues in which you think A and B do not know each other well. How did they meet?

Try to situate each dialogue physically. Where might it be taking place?

What do you think A and B were doing before they met?

In each case a question is being asked about the time, but is A always interested in knowing what time it is? Suggest in each case why A asks about the time. If he is not really asking about the time, what is he doing?

Pick out the dialogues in which B does not seem to know why A is asking the time. If you were B, how would you continue the conversation with A?

Some useful ways of asking

All typical question forms, including WH-questions and HOW ...

Can ...?

May ...?

Could ...?

Do ...?

Have ...?

Is ...?

Would ...?

Production

When we ask about the time, we do not always want to know exactly what time it is. Think of other possible reasons for asking the time when you really want to say something else (e.g. 'Don't you think we ought to be leaving?'). Work these out with a partner and present them in the form of a short sketch to other pairs. They should decide who you are and what you are really trying to say to your partner.

1.6 Why was that, then?
(Seeking clarification)

1   A: *But surely, if he'd had it he'd have used it?*
    B: *Not necessarily . . .*
    A: *He's been there before, hasn't he?*
    B: *Not at night.*
    A: *I don't see that it makes much difference, do you?*
    B: *Well, it depends . . .*

2   A: *Ben?*
    B: *Uh?*
    A: *I don't understand . . .*
    B: *Just wait . . .*
    A: *But he had it with him, din' he?*
    B: *Who?*
    A: *Him – that one!*
    B: *Well, if he'ad it, why din' he use it? Ben?*

3   A: *Oh yes, he always kept it on him.*
    B: *He couldn't have left it somewhere?*
    A: *I doubt it. It's not the sort of thing people leave lying around.*
    B: *It's strange – I must say. And he had it when he left?*
    A: *As far as I know, yes.*
    B: *That means you didn't actually see it?*
    A: *Ohh . . .*

4   A: *That's stupid!*
    B: *What?*
    A: *I had it – only a moment ago . . . At least, I thought it . . .*
    B: *Try the other pocket.*
    A: *No, it's not there.*
    B: *It must be – try the lining!*
    A: *You did give it to me, didn't you?*

Interpretation

Listen to the voices of A and B. Do they sound happy? Worried?
Angry? Thoughtful?
In which dialogue do A and B know each other least well?
Where do you think each dialogue takes place?
What is 'it' in each case?
In dialogues 1, 2 and 3, 'it' belongs to another person. Who is that
other person? What is his relation to A and B?

Some useful ways of seeking clarification

You did ... didn't you? ... Didn't he?
He was, wasn't he? ... Weren't they?
Could he not have ...? ... Couldn't he?
Maybe he ...? ... Isn't it? etc.
Surely you could have ...? Why was that?
I don't understand why ...
Why did you ...?
What was the reason for ...-ing?
It's not clear to me why ...

Production

Each person in the group should think of an unfortunate incident in
which trouble occurs because of somebody's carelessness (e.g. a
friend phones from your flat and does not put the phone back
properly. As a result, you do not receive an important call). Now,
each person should write his incident on a slip of paper. The slips
should be put in a box and each member of the group should draw
one. Now, everyone should go round and try to find out as much as
possible about what happened to the others, and why.

Part two:
Expressing and finding out about
intellectual attitudes

2.1 Yes, but...
(Agreement and disagreement)

1   A: *I suggest we charge a small . . . er . . . fee.*
      B: *I'm not sure that I agree.*
      A: *But we can't just give them away!*
      B: *Why not? We're not paying for them.*
      A: *I know, but . . .*
      B: *But?*
      A: *Well, people like to pay for what they get.*

2   A: *. . . I don't care, but they must pay something.*
      B: *Why should they? What are they getting out of it?*
      A: *Useful experience.*
      B: *Oh, come off it! Useful – like hell!*
      A: *I think you're wrong, but . . . Anyway, what are they putting into it?*
      B: *That's not the point. We can't ask them to pay, and that's that.*

3   A: *Well, they can all bring something.*
      B: *Oh, we can't ask them to do that.*
      A: *Why not? They're all coming, aren't they?*
      B: *But they're our guests!*
      A: *So what? Nobody's forcing them to come.*

4   A: *In my opinion it may be necessary to charge for participation.*
      B: *I'm not sure that would be wise.*
      A: *We have to cover our costs, you know.*
      B: *I know, but there are other ways.*
      A: *Like?*
      B: *Like calling for voluntary contributions.*
      A: *I doubt if that would work.*

Interpretation

What age do you think the speakers are?
In which dialogue do you think they know each other best?
What jobs do you think they have?
Try to situate the dialogues. Where are the characters speaking?
How long have they been there? Are there any other people present?
In each case there is a disagreement. What is the cause of this
disagreement? What are A and B probably talking about?
In most of the dialogues, other people are referred to. Who are
these people?
Imagine that in each case, A wins the argument. How will B explain
to the 'other people' what they have to pay or bring? Will he
contact them personally? By phone? By letter?

Some useful ways of expressing agreement and disagreement

Yes.	No.
That's right.	No, it isn't/wasn't.
You're right.	But (it can't be) . . .
Quite right.	You're wrong.
All right.	It certainly isn't/wasn't.
Absolutely.	I never . . .
Yes it is, isn't it . . .?	I don't agree.
I think so too.	That's not true.
I agree.	I did not!

Production

Imagine a third person, C, in each dialogue. He agrees with A. In
most cases, his support makes B more angry. In pairs, rework the
dialogues introducing the new character C. Before you do so,
decide clearly what kind of person he is and what his relation is to
the other two. Exchange your interpretations with others.

2.2 I don't think so
(Agreement and disagreement)

1 A: *Makes you sick!*

B: *I know. And then they say, 'Well, why didn't you say you didn't want it?'*

A: *As if you could know they were going to put a new one in without asking.*

B: *Exactly. They're all the same – always out to fiddle you.*

A: *Yeah, can't trust any of them.*

2 A: *This will have to be stopped.*

B: *I entirely agree.*

A: *Extra charges should not be allowed.*

B: *Of course not.*

A: *And I suggest that we refuse to pay.*

B: *That's just what I wanted to say . . .*

3 A: *It's too much, I mean . . . I mean, it's really too much.*

B: *They've got a nerve!*

A: *I mean, did I ask them to do it?*

B: *No, of course you didn't.*

A: *So, what right have they got to send me this?*

B: *I dunno, I really don't.*

4 A: *This came in today. I'm going to send it back.*

B: *Good idea.*

A: *I'm not paying a penny.*

B: *No, don't.*

A: *They're a bunch of sharks, they are.*

B: *You're dead right.*

5 A: *I'm not going to pay.*

B: *You're probably right, but . . .*

A: *Look, it isn't my fault, is it?*

B: *Not really.*

A: *So, I'm not going to pay.*

Interpretation

Decide who A and B might be.
Who do you think started each conversation? Why?
What impression do you have of A's character in each case?
A is angry about something. What do you think it is?
Discuss whether B really approves or only pretends to approve of A's attitude.
Why do you think A decided to talk to B? How much is he in fact listening to what B says?
What would happen if B disagreed with A?

Some useful ways of expressing agreement and disagreement

(See unit 2.1)

Production

Why did A refuse to pay? In pairs, decide on a specific reason in each case. As a group, discuss the different reasons given.

2.3   What do you think?

(Inquiring about agreement and disagreement)

1   A: *We'd better tell him now, don't you think?*
    B: *I'm not sure . . .*
    A: *He's going to find out anyway.*
    B: *D'you think so?*
    A: *Well, even if he doesn't, we still* ought *to tell him, surely?*
    B: *I'm not so sure . . .*

2   A: *It's quite obvious he'll have to be told, don't you agree?*
    B: *You know I don't.*
    A: *But if he finds out . . .*
    B: *I think he knows already.*
    A: *Then we've got no choice. We've got to tell him, haven't we?*
    B: *Not necessarily . . .*

3   A: *I think she has a right to know, don't you . . . ? . . . Well, if she hears
       it from someone else, I mean . . . Perhaps . . . Mmm . . . Yes, but it
       must come out sooner or later . . .*

4   A: *We'll tell him tonight. O.K.?*
    B: *No . . . no, no. Let's wait.*
    A: *For what?*
    B: *Maybe he'll . . .*
    A: *Not a chance!*

Interpretation

Who is the person A and B are talking about?
Who are A and B, and what is their relation to this person?
Who is A talking to in dialogue 3?
Where are A and B?
How long do you think they have been there?
Where is the person they are talking about?
What do you think A wants to tell this other person?
Why is B reluctant to tell him?
In dialogue 4, what do you think B was going to say when he began 'Maybe he'll . . .'?
In dialogue 2, what did B have in mind when he said 'not necessarily'?

Some useful ways of inquiring about agreement and disagreement

Don't you think/agree?
Really?
Do you really think so?
I think . . . don't you?
Wouldn't you agree?

O.K.?
All right?
How about it?
What do you say?

Production

Imagine a third person, C, in each dialogue. He agrees with A. In most cases, his support makes B more angry. In pairs, rework the dialogues introducing the new character C. Before you do so, decide clearly what kind of person C is and what his or her relation is to the other two. Then compare your suggestions with others.

Writing

Imagine that B manages to persuade A not to *tell* the third person, but to *write* to him or her. Depending on who you think A is, and what his relation is to the third person, write the communication A would make in each case. Would it be a telegram? A letter? A note? A report? A memorandum? A telex? etc.

2.4 No, I didn't
(Denial)

1 A: . . . *Well you told me to soak it in hot water* . . .
   B: *No I did not!*
   A: *I even wrote it down.*
   B: *I said nothing of the sort. I told you to* dip *it in* warm *water.*
   A: *That's what I did.*
   B: *But you've just said that I told you* . . .

2 A: *I see . . . yes . . . yes I remember, it was Tuesday, wasn't it . . . Oh, really . . . Warped! . . . Ah–ha . . . Ah, yes, but I warned you not to immerse the whole surface . . . No, in fact I said 'sprinkle lightly if necessary' . . . I'm sorry about that, but I'm quite sure I'd never have told you to soak it. You see* . . .

3 A: *Look, it's gone all yellow* . . .
   B: *And you watered it regularly?*
   A: *Every day.*
   B: *At what time?*
   A: *Oh, usually just before lunch.*
   B: *But that's exactly what I told you not to do.*
   A: *Oh? . . . I don't myself remember that. Of course, I might be mistaken* . . .
   B: *I am quite sure I never told you to water it during the heat of the day. Quite sure.*

4 A: *I left them in the solution, like you said.*
   B: *I didn't tell you to leave them in the solution.*
   A: *You did, you know.*
   B: *I certainly did not!*
   A: *If you don't believe me, ask him.*
   B: *Well?*
   C: *That's what you said.*
   B: *That is not what I said. I told you to leave the first lot in the solution, not these ones!*
   C: *Oh . . . the first lot?*

Interpretation

What is the relationship between B and A? What are their jobs? Do they like each other? Where are they?

In which dialogues does A seem to be superior to B?

In each dialogue, B had instructed A to do something. What was that?

From what you have decided about A's character in each case, discuss why he made a mistake. Does A admit that the fault is his?

Some useful ways of expressing denial

No.

No, I didn't/No I did *not*!

Never!

That's not true.

That's a lie.

That's not what I said/meant/intended.

Production

A series of twenty or more portraits will be needed. These should be numbered. In pairs, choose faces to fit the characters in each dialogue. Note the numbers next to the dialogues, then compare your choice with that of others.

Writing

Imagine A has to send a telegram to B explaining what has gone wrong (and asking what to do!). Write one telegram for each dialogue. Remember that each word costs 15p!

2.5 Delighted
(Accepting an offer or invitation)

1 A: *Here, let me . . .*
  B: *Oh no no no – I insist . . .*
  A: *No, really . . .*
  B: *No no – put it away.*
  A: *Please, just this once . . .*
  B: *All right . . .*

2 A: *Well, what's it come to?*
  B: *Hm? Oh no – leave it to me.*
  A: *No no – please. It was my idea.*
  B: *Doesn't matter.*
  A: *Look, I can't possibly let you . . .*
  B: *Well . . . if you're sure . . . thanks very much.*

3 A: *This one's on me, all right?*
  B: *Look, there's no need . . .*
  A: *But I want to.*
  B: *Some other time. O.K.?*
  A: *No, you always say that . . . Please . . .*
  B: *If you really insist . . .*

4 A: *Oh no, it's our turn this time . . .*
  C: *Yes, you can put that away . . .*
  B: *No, we can't possibly . . .*
  D: *No, really, it's far too much . . .*
  A: *Well, then, why don't we split it?*
  C: *Good idea.*
  B: *No, while you're with us . . .*
  D: *Oh yes, this is our pleasure . . .*
  A: *Well, it's really very kind of you . . .*
  C: *Thank you so much.*

Interpretation

Where do you think the dialogues take place?
How well do the people know each other?
How long have they been there?
What is A offering to do in each case?
How is his offer accepted? Willingly? Grudgingly? Gratefully?
What reasons could A have for making his offer?
In dialogue 4, what do you think are the relations between A and
C? B and D?

Some useful ways of accepting an offer or invitation

Thank you very much.
Thanks a lot.
(Many) thanks.
It's very good/kind of you.
You're most kind.
With pleasure.

I'd love to/be glad to.
Delighted.
Yes, please.
All right.
I'm most grateful.

Production

Listen to the tape again. What do you imagine B looks like?
Working in groups of five or six, tell each other as clearly as you
can what you think.

2.6 Sorry, I can't
(Declining an offer or invitation)

1   A: *Who? ... Oh, yes, of course I remember ... Well, that's very kind of you ... Yes, we'd love to, thanks very much ... Yes ... yes ... Yes, it sounds very interesting ... Uh-huh ... Well, I don't think we'll be able to make the lecture, but we should be in time for the reception ... Yes, we'll certainly try ...*

2   A: *On what?*
       B: Communicative competence.
       A: *At what time?*
       B: Six o'clock.
       A: *Look, thank him very much. Tell him we're most grateful and all that ... Unfortunately, we'll be a bit late, but ... we hope to see him afterwards.*
       B: *Anything else?*
       A: *No, I don't think so.*

3   A: *Sounds awfully interesting ...*
       B: *Well, come along if you like.*
       A: *Thanks very much. When did you say it was?*
       B: *Friday, at six.*
       A: *At six ... That's a bit awkward, I'm afraid.*
       B: *I'll be doing another one on Saturday.*
       A: *Saturday? Hm. That's very kind of you. I'll definitely try and make it on Saturday, but if not ... I'll come as soon as I can on Friday.*

4   A: *I certainly don't want to go. Do you?*
       B: *Not very much.*
       A: *Can't we just send a note saying we can't go?*
       B: *But we've already said yes.*
       A: *Why not phone him up later and say we're terribly sorry but it won't be possible for us to come this time ...*
       B: *That's exactly what we said last time.*

Interpretation

Who is A talking to in each dialogue?
In dialogues 1, 2 and 3, how well do A and B know each other?
In dialogue 4, whom do you think A and B are talking about?
In dialogues 1, 2 and 3, suggest how the conversation began. Where are the speakers? How did they get there? Who spoke first?
In dialogue 4, suggest how the conversation is going to end. What will A or B decide to do?
In each dialogue, decide whether A really wants to go or not. If he does not, what is his reason?
In dialogue 1, suggest what the other person is saying.

Some useful ways of declining an offer or invitation

No thank you	It's very kind of you, but . . .
I'd rather not	What a pity, I shan't be (free,
I'm afraid I can't/won't be able	able to come, etc.)
(to) . . .	I regret that I shall not be able to
Unfortunately, I'm/it's	accept . . .

Production

In dialogue 2, suggest what B is going to say to 'him'.
In dialogue 3, suggest a continuation in which B tries to get A to give a more definite answer. Discuss your decisions with at least five others in the class.

2.7 Can I help?
(Making an offer)

1   A: *You seem to be having some problems.*
    B: *It's all right, thanks, I'll manage.*
    A: *Perhaps I could translate for you.*
    B: *That's very kind of you, but I think I'd better explain it myself.*
    A: *Shall I ask him if he's understood you properly?*
    B: *It's very kind of you indeed, but he knows what I want . . .*
    A: *Well, if you're sure I can't help.*
    B: *No, really. Thank you very much.*

2   A: *Can I help?*
    B: *Oh, thank God you're here.*
    A: *What's the matter?*
    B: *He doesn't understand what I want!*
    A: *Would you like me to explain?*
    B: *Please do!*

3   A: *Is there anything I can do to help you?*
    B: *Oh no, we're all right. Thank you very much.*
    A: *Are you quite sure?*
    B: *Well, this man seems to be very upset about something.*
    A: *Shall I see if I can find out what the matter is?*
    B: *Oh, we wouldn't like to put you to any trouble . . .*
    A: *No trouble at all . . .*

4   A: *D'you need help?*
    B: *Looks like it. He doesn't want to understand me.*
    A: *Want me to try?*
    B: *If you like. But I don't think he'll listen to you either.*
    A: *Shall I get Sasha?*
    B: *Good idea.*

Interpretation

First, decide in each dialogue where B is and who he was talking to before A came.

Who is B? Does A know him?

How old are B and A?

What does B feel when he sees A?

What was happening before these dialogues began?

In dialogue 1, why do you think B refuses A's offer of help?

In dialogue 3, why do you think B at first refuses A's offer of help?

Some useful ways of making an offer

May I/can I help?

Do you need (any) help?

Do you want me to . . .?

Would you like me to . . .?

Perhaps I could . . .?

If you like, I'll . . .

(Why don't you) let me . . .

Allow me/permit me to . . .

Can I/shall I . . .?

I'll . . . if you like.

I'll help you.

Production

Divide into large groups. One group should draw up a list of situations, e.g. carrying heavy bags at a crowded railway station, trying to get your car out of the mud, stuck in a foreign town with no money, etc. The other group should draw up a list of characters, giving age, sex, profession, and details such as 'you are in a hurry', 'you have a bad back', 'you are very tired', 'you know nothing about cars', etc.

Each person in the group will have his list of situations or characters. Those with the situations should go to different parts of the room. The characters should then approach (or try to avoid!) them and offer help or be asked for assistance. Situations and characters should be changed several times.

2.8 Let me
(Making an offer)

1   A: *Well, it's right inside, you see . . .*
    B: *D'you want me to have a look?*
    A: *It's very kind of you. but there's a man coming round soon.*
    B: *Oh, well if you have any more trouble, just let me know.*
    A: *We will. Thanks very much.*

2   A: *No, we didn't want to fiddle with it ourselves.*
    B: *Quite right. Now, let's have a look.*
    A: *Perhaps we should wait till we can get someone in . . .*
    B: *Oh, I'll fix that. Don't you worry.*
    A: *The thing is we can't take any risks . . .*
    B: *Don't you worry. I'll be careful.*

3   A: *What's wrong?*
    B: *It won't work.*
    A: *Let's see . . . Oh, that's nothing. I'll do it for you.*
    B: *Thanks, but I'd rather take it back.*
    A: *What for? You're just throwing your money away. I can do it now, if you like.*
    B: *Thanks all the same, but it's not mine you know . . .*

4   A: *I'm afraid I know nothing about these things.*
    B: *I don't know much myself, but I could try . . .*
    A: *Do you think so?*
    B: *If you like.*
    A: *Oh, I'd be most grateful.*
    B: *Then I'll see what I can do.*

Interpretation

What connection is there between A and B? Are they related? Business acquaintances? Neighbours? Friends?
Where do the conversations take place?
What, in each case, do you think is being discussed?
What is B offering to do?
Judging by tone of voice and manner of speaking, try to draw up a short character sketch of A and B in each case. Are they nervous? Friendly? Slow-thinking? Shy? Domineering? etc.
In which dialogue is A most eager to accept help? And least?
In dialogue 1, what had B just said before A's remark 'Well, it's right inside, you see'?
In dialogue 2, what is A trying to tell B when he says, 'Perhaps we should wait till we can get someone in'?
In dialogue 3, what made A ask, 'What's wrong?'?

Some useful ways of making an offer

(See unit 2.7)

Production

As a group, sit down and concentrate, each person thinking to himself of a small object (e.g. a hairpin, a stamp, a splinter). Now split up. Each person should go off and imagine himself having difficulty with that small object (e.g. trying to get a splinter out of his right elbow!). He should work out a simple mime in which it is clear what his problem is. Then he should go round to the others in the group, offering to help them in their difficulty and, in turn, receiving offers of help. In order to help, he must find out what the difficulty is. He may ask questions of the person miming, but that person may only nod or shake his head.

The same exercise may be repeated for difficulty with large objects.

2.9 **Don't you remember?**
(Inquiring about remembering)

1   A: *Did you remember to phone him?*
      B: *Of course.*
      A: *Sorry, I was just asking . . . Is he coming?*
      B: *Yes, on his way back.*
      A: *Good. And you gave him the address, didn't you?*
      B: *Oh . . . Damn!*

2   A: *I hope you didn't forget to phone him again.*
      B: *No, I got him this morning. He was just about to leave.*
      A: *Good. Is he going to be there?*
      B: *Yes, he promised to be there, at least for the last two days.*
      A: *He knows where it's being held, I presume?*
      B: *Er . . . oh . . . I'm not sure . . .*

3   A: *And you did remember to phone him, didn't you?*
      B: *That's the second time you've asked me.*
      A: *I just wanted to be sure, that's all.*
      B: *Well now you know. I phoned him and he's coming.*
      A: *And you told him it wasn't here, I hope.*
      B: *You didn't say anything about that!*
      A: *Didn't I? Are you sure?*

4   A: *I don't suppose you phoned him, did you?*
      B: *Who?*
      A: *What's-his-name . . .*
      B: *Grev?*
      A: *That's right.*
      B: *Yes I did.*
      A: *Is he coming?*
      B: *Uh-huh.*
      A: *He knows where to go, doesn't he?*
      B: *'spose so.*

Interpretation

What relation is there between A and B?
Who do you think they are talking about?
In each dialogue, what is A's reason for asking his question?
What is B's reaction in each case? Is he puzzled? Annoyed?
Surprised? Offended?
What do you think the phone call might be about?

Some useful ways of inquiring about remembering

Do/did you remember . . . ?
You do/did remember . . . don't/
didn't you?
Surely you remember . . . ?

Have you forgotten . . . ?
You haven't forgotten, have
you?
What about the . . . ?

Production

You have asked somebody to post an important letter for you, and
you want to be sure he has not forgotten to do so. How would you
ask if he had remembered, if he or she was:
your brother/sister
a colleague (at work)
a neighbour (whom you don't know too well)
a teenager (the son or daughter of a friend)
somebody much older than you (who had offered to do it)?
Discuss this in your groups. Then, in pairs, work out short dialogues
to illustrate the above. Compare your versions with those of others
in the group.

2.10 No go
(Possibility or impossibility)

1 A: *In that!*
   B: *Why not?*
   A: *You'll never make it.*
   B: *But why not?*
   A: *It's madness. You won't last two hours.*
   B: *Well, we're going to try.*

2 A: *I've nothing against his trying.*
   B: *You have, though.*
   A: *I just don't think it can be done, that's all.*
   B: *But why shouldn't he try?*
   A: *No reason at all – but I think he's wasting his time.*
   B: *Well, don't tell him, please . . .*

3 A: *They don't stand a chance.*
   B: *I wouldn't be so sure . . .*
   A: *Just look at them!*
   B: *There's still time . . .*
   A: *Not a chance!*

4 A: *Impossible!*
   B: *But you can't be sure.*
   A: *It is simply not possible. Physically . . . in any way.*
   B: *But nobody's ever tried.*
   A: *That is hardly surprising.*

Interpretation

Who are A and B? Where do you think they are?
What might they be talking about?
In dialogues 2 and 3, who are they talking about?
In each dialogue, A is trying to get B to change his mind. Why is he doing this?
What circumstances do you think led up to this conversation? Why did it take place?

Some useful ways of expressing possibility or impossibility

It can't be done!
Impossible!
(That's) not possible . . .
I doubt if (it can be done)
I don't think it can be managed.
That can't be done, I'm afraid.
No chance/hope.

It might be possible.
You should be able to . . .
There's no reason why you shouldn't be able . . .
There's a fair chance of . . .
With any luck you'll/we'll/it'll . . .

Production

Think of three people you know well. Imagine how each of them would react to your saying that you intended to:

cycle to a place 5000 kilometres away
take up parachuting as a sport
start studying Chinese
buy a big dog
dye your hair black

(There is no need to change your personality here. If you are unlikely to do any of these things, the remarks of your friends will be all the more interesting.) Compare notes with others in your group.

2.11 Any chance?
(Asking about possibility or impossibility)

1 A: *Can I go too?*
   B: *'fraid not.*
   A: *Can't you say I'm a friend of yours?*
   B: *That would just make it worse!*

2 A: *Would there be any possibility of our representative attending?*
   B: *Not as far as I know.*
   A: *Not even if he were to have an introduction from you?*
   B: *I'm afraid that would be of no help at all.*

3 A: *We will be able to come, won't we?*
   B: *Yes, I think so. Not together, of course.*
   A: *Not even if we say we know you?*
   B: *That won't make any difference, I'm afraid.*

4 A: *Do you mind if I bring a friend?*
   B: *Not at all – but I don't think they'll let him in.*
   A: *What if we got him an invitation?*
   B: *It's far too late, unfortunately.*

Interpretation

Suggest who A and B might be.
What does A want B to do?
What is B's reaction? Is he helpful? Pessimistic? Worried? etc.
What have A and B just been talking about?
What do you think A's next remark will be in each case?
Why does B refuse in each case?

Some useful ways of asking about possibility or impossibility

Can I/we/you ... (+ infinitive form)?

Do you mind if ... (+ infinitive form)?

Will/would you be able to ...?

Do you think we could ...?

Is it possible to ...?

(Is there) any chance of ...?

Production

Imagine in each dialogue that A does not want to accept B's answer. What arguments would he use to try and persuade B to change his mind? Discuss this in your groups. Then, in pairs, work out brief extensions (four lines) to each dialogue, in which A unsuccessfully tries a new approach. Compare your versions with others.

2.12 1+1=2. So...
(Stating logical conclusions)

1 A: *Wait, just let's get it straight: you say he left five hours ago?*
   B: *That's right.*
   A: *Then he should have been here long ago.*
   B: *And he knows the way?*
   A: *He had a map. It was all marked.*
   B: *So he can't have got lost...*
   A: *Unless...*

2 A: *When did he leave?*
   B: *Eight o'clock.*
   A: *Did you check that he had left?*
   B: *Yes, I phoned two hours ago.*
   A: *Then he must be on his way.*
   C: *But if he left at eight, he would have arrived by now.*
   A: *Well, where is he then? We can't wait any longer.*

3 A: *Can you see her?*
   B: *No. Nobody in sight.*
   A: *And when did she leave?*
   B: *Eight o'clock.*
   A: *Are you sure?*
   B: *That's what they told me.*
   A: *That means she had an hour's start on us...*
   B: *So she must be ahead.*

Interpretation

Who are A and B?
Who are they waiting for?
Do you think the person they are waiting for is well known to them?
Where does each dialogue seem to take place?
Why are A and B waiting?
What reasons could there be for the other person being late?
How is the other person expected to come? On foot? By plane? etc.
What do you think A and B will do next?

Some useful ways of stating logical conclusions

If (X), then (Y)   This means that . . .
(and) so . . .   Therefore . . .
Obviously, since . . . (he/she/it)   As a result . . .
must . . .   Consequently . . .
He/she isn't (can't be) . . . because

Production

A number of photographs will be needed, preferably pictures with few distracting details. Pictures showing people in unusual situations or surroundings, or objects being used in an unfamiliar way, are particularly suitable.

One person in each group should take a picture and hold it so that only he can see it. The others, through their questions, should try to work out what is in the picture. They should note carefully what answers are given to the questions and use this information to come to logical conclusions.

Writing

Imagine you are the person A and B were waiting for. You did not meet them. Write a note in which you explain why you were late. Apologise or blame, depending on whose fault it was that you were late.

2.13 Maybe
(Certainty and uncertainty)

1 A: *So he said he'd call for us on Sunday?*
B: *I think it was Sunday. That's 'dimanche', isn't it?*
A: *Uh-huh. But is he coming to us for lunch or are we going to him?*
B: *I suppose he's coming to us . . .*
A: *Anything else you don't quite remember?*
B: *It's not my fault he talks so fast!*

2 A: *Slowly, slowly. Now just say it all again, slowly.*
B: *There's a gentleman who's calling on Sunday who –*
A: *Just a moment. Do you mean phoning or coming round?*
B: *Oh, coming round I should think . . . And he –*
A: *Slow-ly! This Sunday or next?*
B: *I'm really not sure. I don't think he said . . .*
A: *All right. Go on.*
B: *And you're to have lunch with him.*
A: *So he's coming to me so that I can have lunch with him!*
B: *Oh – perhaps it's the other way round. He did say 'chez' something-or-other . . .*

3 A: *No, not Philippe, Gérard . . . no, he didn't, but it must have been Gérard . . . because it sounded like him, that's why. Anyway, he's coming round on Sunday . . . what? . . . I expect so, he didn't say . . . Of course I don't know – I can't ask a thing like that! . . . About one o'clock I should think . . . Quite sure. Philippe's much easier to understand on the phone.*

Interpretation

Suggest who A and B are.

Are they closely related or not? What is their connection?

Who is the man they are talking about?

And what is their relation to him?

There is clearly a misunderstanding between A and B. What is the reason for it?

What is B trying to find out from A?

In dialogue 3, who is A speaking to? What is being said at the other end of the line?

Some useful ways of expressing certainty and uncertainty

I'm sure . . .	I'm not sure . . .
I think . . .	I doubt if (that) . . .
I suppose . . .	I don't think . . .
(It/he) probably . . .	It's unlikely (that) . . .
Perhaps.	I don't believe . . .
Maybe.	
I'm quite certain.	
There's no doubt that . . .	
(He's/it's) definitely . . .	
There's no hope/chance,	
possibility.	

Production

We are often unsure of things we thought we knew. Divide into pairs. One partner should close his eyes. The other may then question him on simple details of his surroundings, e.g. the shape and disposition of the room, the colour, texture, etc. of his own clothes and those of his partner, the time, the weather, etc. In answering the questions, it is important to indicate how sure you think you are of the facts.

There is a similar exercise involving the whole group: a number of everyday objects are placed on a table and examined by everyone for about two minutes. After this the objects are removed; each person should note down as many details as can be remembered. Later, lists may be compared. (Kim's game.)

2.14 How do you know?
(Asking about certainty and uncertainty)

1   A: *Where!*
    B: *At the Crazy Horse Saloon.*
    A: *But she wouldn't be seen dead in a place like that!*
    B: *It was her, all right . . .*
    A: *But . . . oh, I can't believe it! Her! Are you sure?*
    B: *Well, with hair like that . . .*

2   A: *Oh, that's interesting! . . . Alone?*
    B: *As far as I could see.*
    A: *Where did you say it was?*
    B: *The Crazy Horse.*
    A: *I must say I find that very odd . . . Um . . . Are you absolutely certain*
       it was her?
    B: *Yes . . . Yes, I'm sure.*
    A: *Because we don't want any . . . er . . . You understand? But you are*
       quite sure, are you?
    B: *Quite sure . . . I mean, that hair of hers . . .*
    A: *Hmm . . .*

3   A: *Who? . . . Dora! . . . All by herself . . . Where! . . . Oh, I can't*
       believe it, I really can't . . . You're 'avin' me on, aren't you? . . .
       Mmmm. Mmmm. Yeah that's right, sort of purplish . . . Uh-huh . .
       Well, well . . . Well, I never . . . No, I mean, if you say so . . .
       Mmmm. Mmmm. Well, it's none of my business really . . .

4   A: *Where's she gawn, then?*
    B: *Who's that?*
    A: *Mary-Lou.*
    B: *You tried the Crazy Horse?*
    A: *Listen, I'm asking for Mary-Lou!*
    B: *Like I said, you tried the Crazy Horse?*
    A: *Are you tellin' me I'm gonna find her down there!*
    B: *Go have a look.*
    A: *I hope you're wrong. An' if you are . . .*

Interpretation

Who are A and B?

What is their connection with the woman who was seen at The Crazy Horse?

What kind of woman do you think she is?

What is A's reaction in each case when he hears what B has seen? Does B share A's feelings?

Where do you think the woman was seen?

Was there anything unusual in her being at The Crazy Horse?

Why should A and B be interested in her at all?

Where do you think dialogue 4 takes place?

What is being said at the other end of the line in dialogue 3?

Some useful ways of asking about certainty and uncertainty

Are you (quite, absolutely) sure?
Was it/did you really?
You're quite sure, are you?

You couldn't have been mistaken, could you?
How sure are you?

Production

Imagine you are B. Choose a partner and continue each of the conversations with A, telling him what else made you sure you were not mistaken.

Writing

In not more than 150 words, write a brief outline of the story involving Mary-Lou. Exchange stories with others in your group.

2.15 No choice
(Obligation)

1 A: *Hey, where are you going with that?*
  B: *Upstairs.*
  A: *I'll take it up. Leave it here.*
  B: *I can't. I have to hand it over personally.*
  A: *You can hand it over personally to* me.
  B: *No good. I was told to go upstairs.*

2 A: *Excuse me . . .*
  B: *Yes?*
  A: *I'm sorry, but I can't allow you to go up with that, sir.*
  B: *It's all right, I'm delivering it personally.*
  A: *New regulations, sir. I'm sorry.*
  B: *Look, it is my personal responsibility to hand this over.*
  A: *I understand, sir, but I have to check all incoming parcels.*
  B: *This is not a 'parcel'!*

3 A: *Oh, Mr Featherstone, you don't have to carry that up by yourself. Leave it here. I'll take it.*
  B: *Ah, that's very kind of you, but I must give it to the right person.*
  A: *Can't I do that for you?*
  B: *Thank you very much, Mr Miller, but this is something I have to do myself.*

Interpretation

Suggest who A and B might be.
Do they know each other at all?
Is either of them in a position of authority?
What do you think B is carrying? Is it valuable? Breakable? Small?
Large? Cumbersome? Unusual in any way?
Why is B going upstairs?
Where is he? What does he want to do?
Where do these dialogues take place?

Some useful ways of expressing obligation

I have to (must) . . .   I'm expected to . . .
I'm supposed to . . .   They want me to . . .
I'm being forced to . . .   I'm going to have to . . .
I am obliged to . . .   I can't get out of . . .-ing
It's my duty to . . .

Production

Working in pairs, each partner should think of an action and a
personality. In turn, each should mime his action to the other, who
will through the 'personality' he has chosen, try to prevent his
partner from carrying out the action. The partner performing the
action must make it clear that he is obliged to do what he is doing.
Examples of characters and actions might be:

a doorman (hotel)   breaking a car window to open
a nurse   the door
a cook   taking your shirt/skirt off
a park attendant   making a phone call
an air hostess   parking in front of an entrance
                               doing pressups

2.16 Do I have to?
(Inquiring about obligation)

1 A: *Why are you standing 'ere?*
   B: *Because they told us to.*
   A: *Have we got to stand 'ere, then?*
   B: *I'spose so.*
   A: *But why?*
   B: *Because they told us to.*

2 A: *Excuse me, what are you waiting for?*
   B: *I've no idea. They told us to stand here.*
   A: *Yes, but is it necessary for everyone to stand here?*
   B: *I don't know. Ask them.*
   A: *Excuse me . . . um . . . do we have to queue like this?*
   C: *Yes.*
   A: *Oh, I see . . .*

3 A: *Would you mind telling me why we've been kept waiting like this!?*
   B: *This is the queue.*
   A: *I can see that. And I've had enough of queuing. I want to know what we're waiting for.*
   B: *You are waiting for your turn.*
   A: *But if I don't want to, I don't have to queue here. Am I right?*
   B: *No.*

Interpretation

Try to explain who A and B are (and C in dialogue 2)
Where are they?
What relation, if any, is there between them?
What do you think A is waiting for?
Why does he talk to B?
What is B's reaction to A's questions?
Where has A just come from?
Who are the other people in the queue?

Some useful ways of inquiring about obligation

Do I have/need to?
Must I?
I don't have to, do I?
Have I got to . . .?

Is it necessary to . . .?
Is one required/meant/expected to . . .?

Production

As a group, imagine that you have to draw up a *simple* explanation
of the rules of a game to be printed on the back of the box. First,
call for suggestions of games. The person who suggests the game
should pair off with someone who does *not* know how to play it.
Together, they should work out the rules (in writing), with the
person who does not know how to play questioning his partner
about what has to be done at each stage in the game. At the end, the
group should meet again and listen to the various *rules*. It does not
matter if several pairs choose the same game.

2.17 It's up to you
(Obligation for others)

1   A: *What's got into him, then?*
    B: *I think he was expecting a bit more.*
    A: *He got enough, dammit!*
    B: *Yes, I know . . .*
    A: *Well, I don't have to give him any more, do I?*
    B: *Not if you don't want to.*

2   A: *Yes, I'm sorry about that. We should have explained . . .*
    B: *What?*
    A: *Well, you see, usually one is expected to . . . um . . . well, to give a little more.*
    B: *Oh. And how much is that?*
    A: *It varies, you know . . . Anyway, you don't have to . . .*

3   A: *Oh, no no no. Nothing at all.*
    B: *Are you quite sure?*
    A: *Yes, yes, people often ask . . . You are under no obligation whatsoever to . . .*
    B: *To?*
    A: *Oh, to . . . um . . . give anything more.*

4   A: *It's very kind of you. I . . . something isn't clear . . .*
    B: *May I see . . . ah, yes . . . This is, in fact, optional . . .*
    A: *Well, why do they put it on, then?*
    B: *Yes, that's rather hard to explain . . . It's . . . I think you would say 'for appreciation' . . .*
    A: *And if I don't want to give anything?*
    B: *Oh, nobody can force you . . . It's up to you completely.*

Interpretation

Who is A talking to in each dialogue?

In dialogue 1, whom do you think A and B are talking about?

What kind of person do you think A is in each dialogue? Kind? Irritable? Cautious? etc.

Each dialogue mentions something that A was expected to have done but did not do. What do you think this was?

Why does A decide to talk to B?

In which of the dialogues do you think B is trying to persuade A to change his mind? Why?

Some useful ways of expressing obligation for others

You don't have to . . .

There's no need to . . .

You needn't . . .

It's not necessary to . . .

You're not required to . . .

Nobody can force you to . . .

You're under no obligation to . . .

You must (have to) . . .

It must be done (finished, etc.)

You'll have to . . .

You're expected to . . .

You'll be required to . . .

They'll make you . . .

Production

In pairs, try to work out the complete setting for each dialogue: where are A and B? Are they standing or sitting? How long have they been there? Is either of them going to leave soon? How will the conversation probably continue? Exchange your interpretations with others.

2.18 What if you refuse?
(Asking about obligation for others)

1 A: *. . . and you aren't allowed to choose where you're sent?*
B: *Not for the first two years.*
A: *You mean, you have to go anywhere in the country?*
B: *More or less.*
A: *And what happens if you refuse?*
B: *You can't refuse.*

2 A: *Yes, I appreciate that, but he particularly wanted to stay in the north.*
B: *That is not possible, I'm afraid.*
A: *But is he obliged to go . . . if he doesn't want to?*
B: *Put it this way, his personal wishes may be taken into account, but he must accept our decision.*
A: *Is he not allowed to refuse?*
B: *Conditions, you see, are the same for all, so . . .*

3 A: *Look, just say you're not going. To hell with them!*
B: *It's not so easy . . .*
A: *They can't push you around like this. You don't have to go, do you?*
B: *I've no choice.*
A: *But they can't force you to go, surely?*
B: *If I refuse, yes.*

4 A: *Very interesting . . . And how long must they stay?*
B: *Two years.*
A: *Two years . . . And are they allowed back after that?*
B: *It depends. We try to encourage them to stay, of course.*
A: *Of course. And I take it that everyone is required to . . . um . . . participate?*
B: *Oh yes, we make no exceptions.*

Interpretation

Who are A and B? What sort of work do you think they do?
Decide in each dialogue how great the age difference is between
them.
In dialogues 1, 2 and 4, what is A questioning B about?
Why do you think he is questioning B?
What does B feel about being questioned? Is he willing to answer
or does he not want to encourage A to ask more questions?
How did these conversations start? Which do you think were
started by A?
For about how long have A and B been discussing the subject?
Which of these conversations is least likely to continue? Why?

Some useful ways of asking about obligation for others

Do you have to . . .?   required/forced to . . .?
Must you?   Is it necessary for you to . . .?
Are you obliged/expected/

Production

A series of portraits, preferably close-up photographs, will be
needed. Take one at random, then look at your portrait and decide
who it might be. Draw up a short 'life' for your 'double', including
schooling, previous jobs, places lived in, etc. After about five
minutes, form pairs, each partner showing the other his portrait
and being interviewed about his life. One of the most important
questions to be asked is what duties that person had in his various
jobs and what things he had to do that he did not like doing.

2.19 Do you mind?
(Giving and seeking permission)

1 A: *Hey Gus, mind if I dump this on you?*
   B: *Not at all.*
   A: *I'll be back around six. All right?*
   B: *Fine by me. I won't be in, myself . . .*
   A: *Then I'll put it in the cellar. O.K.?*
   B: *Sure. As long as nobody opens it!*

2 A: *I should like to leave this here and collect it later.*
   B: *Certainly. Would you mind filling out this slip.*
   A: *There'll be somebody here after six, I take it?*
   B: *Not here, no.*
   A: *Well, could I leave it somewhere else?*
   B: *You could try, but I don't know if anyone would be willing to look after it.*

3 A: *Would you let me leave this here, please?*
   B: *Better ask him.*
   A: *Have you any objection to my leaving this here?*
   C: *Well, it's a bit . . . er . . . unusual, isn't it?*
   A: *Nothing to worry about, though.*
   C: *All right then, but don't be too long.*

4 A: *Oh, no, just small ones . . . Well we didn't have time really. And it was the rainy season . . . No, no we had no trouble at all . . . Mmm. Listen, I was wondering if your mother would let me leave them in her flat this evening . . . Uh-huh . . . Oh no, not like last time, I promise! . . . Well, the bathroom's the best place . . . I see . . . Then can I keep the keys? . . . Fine . . . Many thanks. ' Bye.*

Interpretation

Who are A and B? How well do they know each other? Can you tell anything from A's way of talking to B? Does he respect him? Fear him? Ignore him? Consider him his equal or his inferior? etc.
What do you think A wants to leave in each case? Is there anything unusual about it?
What is B's reaction? Does he find A's request reasonable? Does he want to help A?
Do you think A has ever done this before?
What do you think is being said at the other end of the line in dialogue 4?

Some useful ways of giving and seeking permission

You may/can if you want/like.	May I/Can I?/Could I?
Yes, of course.	Is it all right if . . .?
Certainly.	Do you mind if . . .?
By all means.	Would you object if . . .?
Please yourself.	Would it be possible to . . .?
Go ahead.	If you don't mind, I'd like to . . .
You have my permission.	Have you any objection to my . . .-ing?

Production

Imagine that in each case, B (or C) refused to let A leave whatever he had with him. Write out individually a set of four new dialogues using the same characters. Compare your versions with those of the others in your group.

Writing

In dialogues 1, 3 and 4, imagine that A will not be able to see B personally and will have to send C round with whatever it is he wants to leave. Write the note A would send with C to give to B.

2.20 Do they let you?
(Asking about permission for others)

1   A: *Well, how are you getting on?*
      B: *It's all right, I suppose . . .*
      A: *Do they let you out a bit?*
      B: *Just round the park – when it's fine.*
      A: *And are you allowed to have a drink now and then?*
      B: *Drink! They won't even let you have a cigarette!*

2   A: *What about visitors – are they permitted?*
      B: *Oh yes, once a week. From two to three.*
      A: *That's not much, is it?*
      B: *Quite enough, I feel.*
      A: *And are they allowed to receive parcels?*
      B: *Food, yes. In small quantities. But no drink and no cigarettes. We are very firm on that!*

3   A: *Gloomy, isn't it?*
      B: *You get used to it.*
      A: *What's that you're wearing?*
      B: *They call it a 'house-gown'.*
      A: *Is everyone supposed to wear one?*
      B: *Oh yes – with your number in red.*
      A: *Oh, hell . . . When do they let us out?*
      B: *Sundays, sometimes . . .*
      A: *How do you get a drink, then?*
      B: *Drink!*
      A: *Don't tell me they won't let us have a drink.*
      B: *What d' you think you've come to?!*

Interpretation

Who do you think A and B are? Are they strangers? Friends?
Colleagues? Old acquaintances?
Where do you think these conversations are taking place?
Why are A and B talking together? How much longer will the
conversation last?
Is dialogue 2 in any way different from 1 and 3?
In dialogue 2, what do you think A and B had been discussing
before A's question 'What about visitors'?

Some useful ways of asking about permission for others

Are you allowed to ...?   Has anyone said you can/
Do they let you ...?   may ...?
Can you ...?   Did anyone give you permission
Is it possible for you to ...?   to ...?
Do you have permission to ...?

Production

Think of a profession, preferably one which involves special
discipline. Working in pairs, interview each other, trying to find out
what each is allowed and not allowed to do in his profession.

2.21 No, you can't!
(Refusing permission)

1
- A: *Look, the answer is 'no'!*
- B: *But why?*
- A: *I've told you. You're too young.*
- B: *I'm eighteen.*
- A: *I won't let you. It's a mad idea.*
- B: *Why? Because it's one of mine?*

2
- A: *Yes. Yes, we have . . . Your request has not been accepted.*
- B: *But why not? They're letting the others do it.*
- A: *No reason is given. But permission will not be granted.*
- B: *Then I'd like to speak to the Head of the Commission.*
- A: *That, I'm afraid, is not possible.*
- B: *I should like an* official explanation.
- A: *In that case, you should make a written request.*

3
- A: *Did you talk to him?*
- B: *Yes.*
- A: *What did he say?*
- B: *He refused even to consider it.*
- A: *But if Alexis can . . .*
- B: *That's different.*
- A: *But didn't he give any reason?*
- B: *No, just 'regulations are regulations' – as usual.*

4
- A: *Well?*
- B: *She won't let you.*
- A: *Who the hell does she think she is?!*
- B: *I've never seen her so angry. She said: 'Tell him I never want to see him in here again! And if . . .'*
- A: *All right, all right. Don't go on.*

Interpretation

Who are A and B?
In dialogues 3 and 4, they are speaking of someone else. Who do you think that person is?
What do you think A has been asking about?
What does B think of A's request in each case?
How many times do you think A has made his request?
What will A probably do next?
In dialogue 4, what do you think A did to have made the woman so angry?

Some useful ways of refusing permission

You may not.
You can't.
You're not allowed to.
It will not be allowed.
I'm refusing . . .

Permission will not be granted.
. . . is forbidden.
I won't let you.
I will not permit . . .
No, you may not.

Production

Discuss occasions in your life when you have not been allowed to do something. What was the reason given? How was it given? Who told you? Did you protest? Did you try again?

Writing

After deciding what A's request was, write notes or letters of protest to the person who made the decision in dialogues 2, 3 and 4.

Part three:
Expressing and finding out about emotional attitudes

3.1 **Mmm!**
(Pleasure or liking)

1 A: *Oh, very much indeed!*
   B: *You aren't bored?*
   C: *Not at all.*
   B: *Perhaps you would like to stop for a little?*
   A: *Well . . . I . . . don't know about you? . . .*
   C: *It might be a good idea . . . just for a while.*

2 A: *But I am enjoying myself!*
   B: *You don't look like it.*
   A: *I'm concentrating, that's all.*
   B: *Don't you want to stop for a while?*
   A: *No, no. Let's go on . . . It's great.*
   B: *Alright, then. On we go . . .*

3 A: *Yes, it really is most interesting.*
   B: *You're not too tired?*
   A: *Oh no. Not at all. It's most enjoyable.*
   B: *Please let me know if you would like to stop.*
   A: *Well, perhaps this wouldn't be a bad moment . . .*

4 A: *Yes, do go on . . .*
   B: *Well, just one or two more, perhaps . . .*
   C: *I don't know how you do it . . .*
   A: *Yes, you really are very good . . .*
   B: *I hope I am not keeping you . . .*
   A: *Oh, no. Don't worry . . .*
   C: *Yes, we're quite happy . . .*
   B: *Well, you'll let me know if I go on too long, won't you?*

Interpretation

In each of the dialogues, try to decide how well the speakers know each other. How old are they? What sort of people are they? Where is each dialogue taking place?
What do you think the subject of their conversation is?
Are any of the people in any of the dialogues being insincere? Which?

Some useful ways of expressing pleasure or liking

(It's/he's) lovely!
Very nice/wonderful/marvellous/fascinating/delightful.
Great.
I've very much enjoyed . . .
I liked . . . a lot.
We were so pleased/happy to be able to . . .
It was such an interesting/pleasant/enjoyable . . .
It was so pleasant/enjoyable/etc. . . . .
What an interesting/enjoyable/etc. . . . .
How lovely/nice/wonderful . . .
That was wonderful/great/etc. . . . .

Production

In your groups, choose one of the dialogues and discuss what might have been said immediately before it. This should not take longer than ten minutes. When you have decided, send one member of your group to another group to tell them your idea.

Think of situations in which you may have been bored but had to pretend you were enjoying yourself. What did you do or say? Use one of these situations to work out a brief dialogue with a partner.

Writing

Choose one of these dialogues to work on. Imagine that you are writing to a friend about this incident. What will you say in your letter?

3.2 Ugh!
(Displeasure or dislike)

1   A: *Well?*
    B: *Hell!*
    A: *Was it that bad?*
    B: *Pretty awful.*
    A: *What happened?*
    B: *Nothing.*
    A: *No. Seriously?*
    B: *Nothing. We just sat round in a circle . . .*
    A: *Doing what?*
    B: *Thinking, I suppose.*

2   A: *Well, how did you find it?*
    B: *Oh, very interesting . . . Yes . . . Very interesting.*
    A: *Of course, every time we learn a bit more.*
    B: *Yes . . . Yes . . . I'm sure.*
    A: *Well – hope to see you again next week.*
    B: *Oh, yes. I'll do my best to be there.*

3   A: *What was your impression?*
    B: *I thought it was very poor.*
    A: *Really? Why?*
    B: *Well, he's a fraud to start with. I didn't like his approach at all.*
    A: *You mean the er . . . ?*
    B: *Not just that. The whole atmosphere. It irritated me.*

4   A: *Well we were a bit disappointed, I must say. Of course, you never
        quite know what to expect from these sort of things, do you? But we'd
        heard so much about it, and . . . well . . . I didn't really enjoy myself
        very much . . . Hm? . . . No, I suppose one isn't meant to enjoy
        oneself really. That's the whole principle, isn't it? Still, I don't think
        I care for it very much . . .*

Interpretation

What sort of people are A and B? How old might they be?
Do you think A or B in any of the dialogues tends to exaggerate?
Where are A and B at the moment?
Where has B just come from?
What has B been doing? Was A with him or not?
In dialogue 4, why does A say 'these sort of things'?
Why does he not mention precisely what these things are?
In dialogue 2, what does B mean by 'interesting'?
Was it really interesting? If not, what is B avoiding through these words?
What is being said at the other end of the line in dialogue 4?

Some useful ways of expressing displeasure or dislike

I didn't like/enjoy/think much of/care for ...
It was absolutely dreadful/awful/terrible/lousy/shocking/ etc.
I must say, I thought it was very poor/disgraceful/no good/etc.
What I didn't like/care for/appreciate was ...
That was the worst ... I've ever ...
Rotten.
No good at all.
Terrible.
Pointless.
A waste of time.
Ridiculous.
Very bad/poor/weak/etc.

Production

Often, when we are disappointed, we do not want to hurt someone else's feelings by saying so directly. Discuss in your group the occasions in the last few weeks when you have tried to soften your disappointment. Who were you talking to? What did you say? The others in the group should criticise you if they think you have been too weak (or hypocritical!); they should suggest what they feel you ought to have said.

Writing

Take two of the dialogues. Imagine that A cannot talk to B, and therefore sends him a brief note telling him what happened.

3.3 Well?
(Asking about likes or dislikes)

1 A: *You know what this is, I'm sure . . .*
   B: *Um . . .*
   C: *Oh, isn't it, er . . .*
   A: *Yes, I thought you might like something familiar.*
   B: *Oh, yes . . .*
   A: *It's funny, it took me a long time to get to like it . . .*
 • C: *Oh?*
   A: *But now I'm very fond of it . . . Of course, it's nothing special . . .*
   B: *Oh, no, it's . . . very good.*
   A: *I thought you'd like it . . . And how about you? How do you find it?*
   C: *Oh, I agree with Sasha, it's really . . .*

2 A: *Well, could you let us know what he doesn't like?*
   B: *Oh, he's very easy to please.*
   A: *Yes, but we don't want any problems. Are you sure there isn't anything else he doesn't like?*
   B: *No, apart from what I told you yesterday.*

3 A: *. . . but can't you tell me a bit more about him? . . . I know I'll be seeing him, but I don't know what to give him . . . What d'you mean 'anything'? . . . But he might not like it . . . No, I just want to know what he likes and what he doesn't like . . . Well you ought to know . . . Then just tell me something he's fond of . . . Oh . . . Well, I'll try . . .*

Interpretation

For each of the dialogues say who you think the characters are. Give their age, occupation or social role, their relationship to the other person, etc.

Where is each of the dialogues taking place?

What is the thing the people are talking about in each dialogue?

Who is A talking to in dialogue 3?

In dialogue 2, A says 'Yes, but we don't want any problems'. What does this tell you about his relationship with B?

What do you think the other person is saying in dialogue 3?

Some useful ways of asking about likes and dislikes

How would you/he like it . . .?

Does he like . . .-ing?

Is there anything he especially enjoys/hates . . .-ing?

Could you tell me whether there's anything he particularly likes/ dislikes . . .-ing?

What do you think he would like/enjoy . . .-ing?

Do you think he'd like it/mind if I . . . ?

What about . . .? Would he like that or not?

Production

Take dialogue 2 and discuss in pairs how this conversation might have started and how it might continue. Write down this longer dialogue, then change partners and discuss your different versions.

Suppose that in dialogue 1, B and C had been unwilling to accept the thing that is being talked about. What might they have said? How would the dialogue be changed?

3.4 Really!
(Surprise)

1   A: *They've found it!*
    B: *No! Where?*
    A: *On top of a six-storey building.*
    B: *Impossible!*

2   A: *It's been found.*
    B: *Really!*
    A: *At least, part of it has.*
    B: *Oh. Where?*
    A: *On top of Broadcasting House.*
    B: *What on earth was it doing there?*

3   A: *We know where it is!*
    B: *Do you?*
    A: *Aren't you pleased?*
    B: *Oh, yes . . . Well, where is it?*
    A: *Just across the street – on the top floor of that building.*
    B: *That's odd.*
    A: *Why?*
    B: *Because I found it yesterday – in the cellar!*

4   A: *They've found it at last!*
    B: *Great! Where is it?*
    A: *On top of a building.*
    B: *How the hell did it get up there?!*
    A: *No idea. But I don't know how we're going to get it down.*

5   A: *It's turned up at last.*
    B: *Yes, I know.*
    A: *You know!?*
    B: *Yes, it's on top of Broadcasting House.*
    A: *But you can't possibly have known. Unless . . .*
    B: *Unless? . . .*

Interpretation

In which dialogue do the people know each other best? Least?
In which dialogue is the person most surprised?
What is the thing which has been found?
Where is each of the dialogues taking place?
In dialogue 5, what do you think A was going to say after
'unless . . .'?

Some useful ways of expressing surprise

Oh! Oh, no!
Really!
What! (and all question words
in exclamatory form)
Impossible!
Incredible!
Really!
I can't believe it!
You must be joking!

Well, how about that!
Well I never!
You don't say!
Good God!/Heavens!
Well, this *is* a surprise!
Did you really!
Have they really!
Surely not!
Honestly!

Production

In pairs, discuss how at least one of the dialogues might have
continued. Then change partners and discuss your different versions.

Writing

Come to an agreement with your group about the precise nature of
the incident in the dialogue. Then write a brief newspaper article
describing it.

3.5 Aah yes!
(Satisfaction)

1 A: ... *and this one?*

B: *Hm? No. No, that won't do.*

A: *Too dark?*

B: *Too lifeless.*

A: *And this?*

B: *Ah, that's better! Just what I wanted. Is it one of yours?*

A: *No, not this one I'm afraid.*

2 A: ... *any better?*

B: *Yes ... yes, there is an improvement.*

A: *I could do another one if you like.*

B: *No, don't worry. That'll do.*

3 A: *Oh, you shouldn't listen to him! ... No, no, they're excellent. Couldn't be better ... Yes, but nobody's perfect ... Oh, I shouldn't worry about a thing like that. You know, it gives them a sort of, um, misty quality, like what's-his-name, you know, the one who does the girls-in-the-country stuff ... yes ... well I certainly like them ...*

4 A: *No, we're quite pleased with his work.*

B: *He thought you weren't.*

A: *Really?*

B: *I like what he does ...*

A: *I wish you'd tell him that. He's feeling a bit low ...*

B: *I have told him, you know, but I don't think he believes me.*

Interpretation

For each dialogue, say who you think the characters are (their age, job, relationship, etc.).

Where is each dialogue taking place?

What is the subject of the conversation?

How would you describe A's attitude in dialogue 2?

What is the attitude of the speakers to each other in dialogue 4?

In dialogue 3, what is being said at the other end of the line?

Some useful ways of expressing satisfaction

It's very good/fine/absolutely right/perfect.

That's just what I wanted/fine/great/etc.

It couldn't be better.

I think it's a great improvement/much better/just right/etc.

Well, isn't that lovely/great/etc.!

I'm very pleased/happy/satisfied/etc. with . . .

I don't think I've ever . . . (heard seen etc.) . . . anything quite so good.

That's good.

Production

Discuss with your group what the people in the dialogues might have been saying to each other just before. Write this out as an addition to *one* of the dialogues, then discuss it with another group. In dialogue 4, what do you think B goes on to say after 'really . . .'?

3.6 That won't do
(Dissatisfaction)

1   A: *But that's not green, it's turquoise!*

    B: *You didn't say what kind of green you wanted.*

    A: *Well . . . a . . . green green. I don't see what's so difficult about that.*

    B: *This was all I could get. It'll do, won't it?*

    A: *No, it won't. It doesn't go at all! Look . . .*

2   A: *And what's all this?*

    B: *That's the sky . . . and that's the grass.*

    A: *But that's no good. You've got them upside down.*

    B: *Why?*

    A: *Well, the sky's green and the grass is blue.*

    B: *Because I'm standing on my head.*

3   A: *This is the undercoat, is it?*

    B: *No, that's the finish. Microvinyl – doesn't need an undercoat.*

    A: *But where did you get that dreadful colour?*

    B: *You said you wanted the two greens mixed.*

    A: *I know . . . but this isn't what I had in mind at all. At all.*

    B: *Well, it's a bit late to start changing it now, in't it?*

4   A: *How do you like it?*

    B: *It's come out . . . very well, I think. I suppose you'll tone down the . green?*

    A: *No. Tone it down?*

    B: *Don't you find it a bit . . . gaudy?*

    A: *No. Not at all. Of course, if you don't like it . . .*

    B: *No, I do. No, really. It's . . . it's probably just the light . . .*

Interpretation

In which dialogues are the speakers most rude to each other? And most polite?
In which one do they know each other best?
What are the relationships between speakers in each dialogue? (i.e. friend to friend, husband to wife, customer to tradesman, etc.).
Where is each of the conversations taking place?
In dialogue 4, what does A really mean when he says, 'I suppose you'll tone down the . . . green?'? And what does B really mean when he says, 'Of course, if you don't like it . . .' in the same dialogue?
What is the green thing in each dialogue?

Some useful ways of expressing dissatisfaction

Awful/dreadful/disgraceful/hopeless/disgusting/rotten.
No good at all/not what we wanted/not up to scratch.
I'm not satisfied with/happy about . . .
I can't say I liked/felt happy about/was satisfied with . . .
It won't do/isn't good enough/is not satisfactory.
That's very bad.

Production

In pairs, discuss how one of the dialogues might continue if the person who is dissatisfied *insists* on a change in the colour. Write this out, then change partners and compare your different versions.

In our everyday lives, we are very often dissatisfied with the service we get or with the behaviour of others. Note down individually three examples from your own experience, then discuss these with the others in your group. What do you need to say to express your dissatisfaction?

3.7 Oh dear!
(Disappointment)

1 A: *Did you get it?*
   B: *Yes. Here you are.*
   A: *And the hooks?*
   B: *Hooks?*
   A: *Don't tell me you forgot the hooks!*
   B: *Oh, I knew there was something else. It doesn't matter, though . . .*
   A: *Of course it matters.*

2 A: *They've arrived at last, Mr Dawson.*
   B: *Thank goodness for that.*
   A: *Here's the list.*
   B: *Ah-ha . . . Good . . . good . . . ah-ha . . . fine. And the replacements?*
   A: *You mean these?*
   B: *But those are the same ones!*
   A: *They must have sent them back by mistake.*
   B: *Oh, they are infuriating!*

3 A: *Is it ready?*
   B: *Not yet.*
   A: *Well, when's he going to have it done by?*
   B: *He doesn't know.*
   A: *Why not?*
   B: *He can't get a spare part.*
   A: *Oh no, that's the second time!*

Interpretation

Say who you think the people are in each of the dialogues. Give their age, job, status, etc.

What is their relationship to each other?

What is the subject of each dialogue?

Have the speakers been together long?

In dialogue 1, what does A really mean by, 'Don't tell me you forgot the hooks!'?

In the same dialogue A says, 'Of course it matters.' What emotion does this reveal?

Where is each dialogue taking place?

Some useful ways of expressing disappointment

Oh hell/damn!

Oh dear/no!

How disappointing!

I had *so* hoped . . .

It doesn't matter, I suppose.

It can't be helped, I suppose.

What a pity/shame/nuisance/ etc.!

Not again!

I'd been *so* much looking forward to . . .

Oh well . . .

Some other time perhaps.

Production

In pairs, choose a dialogue which might be continued by one of the speakers trying to suggest an alternative course of action or a solution to the problem. When you have finished, change partners and discuss your different versions.

3.8   **What a pity!**
(Disappointment)

1   A: *Who was that?*

   B: *Isabelle.*

   A: *Hasn't she left yet?*

   B: *She says she can't come.*

   A: *Oh, that's maddening. Now what are we going to do?*

2   A: *Isabelle! Good to hear you . . . You can't? . . . Oh, I am sorry . . .*
Of course not, it isn't your fault . . . No, I'm sure we'll find someone
else . . . It's a pity, though, isn't it? . . . Yes, I understand . . . Well,
thanks for letting us know . . .

3   A: *. . . so I won't be able to come, I'm afraid.*

   B: *You're sure you can't make it?*

   A: *I'm sure . . . I'm very sorry . . .*

   B: *So are we.*

   A: *I hope it won't ruin your plans . . .*

   B: *No, no. We'll manage, I suppose.*

   A: *There was nothing I could do.*

   B: *I realise. It's just most unfortunate . . .*

4   A: *I've decided . . . not to come with you.*

   B: *No!*

   A: *I had to, Mike.*

   B: *But why not, Isabelle?*

   A: *I can't . . .*

   B: *If you'd only told me before . . . Not now, when . . .*

   A: *I'm sorry.*

Interpretation

In which dialogue do the speakers express their feelings most openly?
What are the relationships between the speakers in each dialogue?
What do you think is the event referred to in each dialogue?
Are the dialogues taking place outside, or in a building of some kind?
If the latter, what sort of a room is it?
In dialogue 1, what does 'Now what are we going to do?' tell you
about the event which Isabelle cannot come to?
Why do you think A says, 'I had to . . .' in dialogue 4?
If you had to break bad news, which of the people in the dialogues
would you prefer to break it to?
What is B saying at the other end of the line in dialogue 2?

Some useful ways of expressing disappointment

(See unit 3.7)

Production

In pairs, extend one of the dialogues in either direction, before or
after the dialogue given. Change partners and discuss your different
versions.

You probably have a number of interesting or important things
which you expect to happen to you in the next few weeks. Write
these down individually, then pass them round for comment.

Writing

Someone failed to turn up to something you organised last
weekend, and this spoiled the event. Decide what the event was,
then write a letter to the person expressing your disappointment
but concealing your irritation.

3.9 I don't like the look of it
(Fear or worry)

1 A: *If you like, but I think it's unwise to let him out so soon.*
B: *But he must get out sooner or later.*
A: *I'm not sure he's ready, yet.*
B: *Nor am I, to be quite honest, but the longer he stays here the harder it gets.*
A: *You're right, I know. All the same, it worries me.*

2
A: *He must get out.*
B: *Not yet. Please, Fred. Not yet.*
A: *He can't go on staying here.*
B: *Fred, I'm so frightened . . .*
A: *I'll be with him.*
B: *But you never know what might happen.*

3
A: *I'm taking him away.*
B: *Well, I can't stop you.*
A: *You don't approve, do you?*
B: *I can't say that I'm happy about it.*
A: *But look how long he's been here. And what difference has it made?*
B: *It takes a long time, you know . . . But do as you wish.*

4
A: *You'll regret it, you know.*
B: *We'll see.*
A: *He's not ready for it.*
B: *He's as ready as he'll ever be.*
A: *He still needs more time.*
B: *He's had enough time. I'm taking him out.*
A: *I hope you're not making a big mistake.*

Interpretation

Which of the dialogues are between equals and which are between a superior and an inferior?
What can you guess about the jobs or positions that the people occupy in each dialogue?
What sort of place does each dialogue occur in?
Who do you think 'he' is?
Where is he being taken away from?
In dialogue 4, what does A really mean when he says, 'I hope you're not making a big mistake'?

Some useful ways of expressing fear or worry

I'm afraid/frightened/scared/worried.
It worries/scares/frightens me.
I don't like this at all.
It makes me feel uneasy.
I'm not at all happy about . . .
There's something not quite right about . . .
I've got a nasty/strange/uneasy feeling that . . .

Production

In groups, discuss how one of the dialogues could be lengthened. The person who wants to take 'him' away has been persuaded not to, but he will make conditions before he agrees. Write out your extended dialogue and discuss it with another group.

Think of situations in which a person is proposing to do something difficult or dangerous (e.g. fighting a shark underwater). Take turns in telling these to the others in the group. They should reply, showing their fears or worries about you.

3.10 That's much better
(Preference)

1 A: *Are you all right?*
    B: *Yes, thanks, quite all right.*
    A: *Don't you want to come in?*
    B: *No, I'm quite happy out here.*
    A: *Isn't it rather cold?*
    B: *It is a bit, but I can't stand it inside. It's terribly smoky. I'd rather stay here, if you don't mind.*
    A: *Oh, it doesn't worry me.*

2 A: *What about him?*
    B: *Don't worry about him.*
    A: *But he's all by himself.*
    B: *He's all right.*
    A: *He must be terribly cold, though.*
    B: *Leave him. He likes it better outside.*
    A: *Strange . . .*
    B: *He'll come in later.*

3 A: *Do you think it could be held out here?*
    B: *I'm not sure. I'll have to ask about that.*
    A: *We'd be very grateful if you could.*
    B: *But what about the Conference Hall? What's wrong with that?*
    A: *We'd prefer to be outside if possible.*
    B: *Well, it's not going to be easy, but we'll do what we can . . .*

4 A: *. . . too bad if it rains . . . well, I'm inviting them, aren't I? . . . We'll just get wet, that's all . . . I am being serious . . . No, honestly, I'd much rather have it outside . . . because it's not so cramped, that's why . . . and anyway, it's so much nicer . . .*

Interpretation

For each of the dialogues give your opinion on these facts about the speakers: age, profession, mood, attitude to the other person.
Where do you think each of the dialogues is taking place?
In dialogue 1, what does A really mean when he says, 'Oh, it doesn't worry me?' What else might he have said?
In dialogue 3, why do you think A says, 'Do you think it could be held out here?' instead of, 'I want it to be held out here'?

Some useful ways of expressing preference

I think . . .
On the whole . . .
If you don't mind . . .
If it's all the same to you . . .
Perhaps it would be better if . . .
Perhaps the best thing would be
to . . .

I'd rather not . . .
I'd prefer not to . . ./. . .-ing
I like . . . better than . . .

Production

In pairs, work out what the people might have been saying just before one of the dialogues began.

You must have some strong likes. Write down three things you like, then explain to the other members of your group why you prefer these things to others of a similar kind (e.g. why you prefer sea fish to river fish/tennis to squash/etc.).

3.11 Which?

(Asking about preference)

1   A: *What'll you have, then?*

   B: *What've you got?*

   A: *There's this – which you know – and this, which I got from a village, . . . and all the usual stuff . . .*

   B: *I'm not sure.*

   A: *What about the one from the village?*

   B: *Mind if I smell it? . . . I think I'll stick to my usual, thanks.*

2   A: *What can we offer you, then?*

   B: *Oh, I don't mind, really . . .*

   A: *What about you?*

   C: *Oh . . . whatever you've got . . .*

   A: *Well there it is. Take your pick.*

   B: *I can't make up my mind. What are you having?*

   C: *It's all the same to me. What about you?*

   A: *I'm not having anything myself.*

   B: *I don't think I'll have anything either . . .*

   A: *Oh, come on. Don't worry about me.*

   C: *Well, er, what do you suggest?*

   A: *Depends what you like. How about this?*

   B: *It's not terribly strong, is it?*

   A: *Try it. Or would you rather have some of the Japanese stuff?*

   B: *It's so hard to decide. Ben?*

   C: *You haven't got anything . . . um . . . soft, have you?*

   A: *No. Sorry.*

   B: *Then perhaps just a little of that.*

   A: *Which would you prefer, the dry or the semi-dry?*

   B: *Oh, either will do . . .*

   A: *What about you?*

   C: *Me too . . . Whichever's easiest . . .*

Interpretation

In which dialogues do the people know each other best?
What is the thing which is being offered?
How would you describe the character of C in dialogue 2? And A?
Do you think that the place in which dialogue 2 is taking place has an effect on the behaviour of B and C?

Some useful ways of asking about preference

Would you like/rather have/prefer . . .?
How/what about . . .?
Which would you rather have/prefer/like best?
Perhaps you'd like/rather have/prefer . . .?

Production

In pairs, try to work out an ending for dialogue 2 in which B and C are forced to come to a decision.

Writing

Write a letter to a friend setting out alternative dates for spending a weekend together and several alternative ways of spending it. Try to find out what he or she prefers.

3.12 Thanks
(Gratitude)

1 A: *I really don't know how to thank you . . .*
 B: *I'm glad I was able to help.*
 C: *Yes, it's most kind of you . . .*
 A: *I don't know what we'd have done if you hadn't come along.*
 B: *Don't mention it. It was the least I could do.*
 C: *Well, thank you once again. And goodbye.*
 A: *Goodbye, and thank you very much. We're most grateful.*
 B: *It was a pleasure.*
 A: *And if there's ever anything we can do for you . . .*
 C: *Oh yes, don't hesitate to let us know. You've got our address, haven't you? Jim . . .*
 A: *Yes, this is our address. That's my home number – and that's the office. If ever you're passing through . . .*
 C: *Do call us up. We'd be so glad to see you.*
 B: *Thank you very much. I'll certainly . . .*
 A: *Oh, and you must give us your address.*
 C: *I think we have that already . . . Yes, we have. Well, once again. Many thanks.*
 B: *Not at all. I'm glad to have been of help.*
 A: *It really was a great help, you know. Well, it's been a pleasure meeting you . . .*
 C: *Indeed it has, and I hope we meet again.*
 A: *So do I.*
 B: *I'm sure we will. Well, I must be . . .*
 A: *Yes, please don't let us keep you. Goodbye, and –* many thanks.
 B: *You're most welcome.*
 C: *Many thanks indeed. You will look us up, won't you?*
 B: *Certainly.*
 A: *Goodbye then.*
 B: *Goodbye . . .*
 C: *Such a nice man.*
 A: *I don't know what we'd have done without him.*
 C: *We'll have to write and thank him when we get back.*

Interpretation

Do A and C know B well?
What sort of people are they? Rich? Sophisticated?
What are A and C thanking B for?
Do you think B will go to see them one day?
Whereabouts is this conversation taking place?

Some useful ways of expressing gratitude

Thanks/many thanks.
Thanks a lot/thanks very much (indeed).
Thank you very much.
I don't know how to thank you.
You've been most helpful/kind/etc.
It was really very/extremely/terribly/most kind of you.
I'm/we're really/most/very grateful to you.
How can I thank you?
You've been so kind/helpful/etc.
I/we can't thank you enough/tell you how grateful we are.

Production

In groups, work out three fairly unimportant reasons for thanking
someone and three very important ones. Then, in pairs, act out these
situations. Before you start, think about the language you may need.

Writing

Write the letter that A and C spoke of in the last line of the dialogue.

3.13 How kind
(Gratitude)

1 A: . . . *and please tell her how grateful I am.*
B: *I'll do that.*
A: *It was really extremely kind of her.*
B: *I'll tell her when she gets back.*
A: *Please do. Oh, and tell her not to worry about that little bit at the back. I'll have it fixed next week.*

2 A: *I've brought it back; a bit late, I'm afraid.*
B: *Doesn't matter. I didn't need it.*
A: *Good. Well . . . thanks.*
B: *You're welcome.*
A: *Oh, by the way, there's a bit here that seems to have got broken somehow . . .*

3 A: *Oh, I'm sorry. I forgot again. I'll bring it in tomorrow.*
B: *If you would . . .*
A: *Of course, of course. And thank you very much for letting us keep it so long.*
B: *Not at all.*
A: *I'm extremely grateful. Everyone enjoyed it, you know.*
B: *I'm glad.*
A: *Anyway, I'll bring it back tomorrow.*
B: *Thank you.*
A: *And . . . er . . . you do know about the broken bit at the beginning, don't you?*

Interpretation

Put the dialogues in order according to how well the people know each other.

What is A's attitude to 'the broken bit' in each dialogue?

Where do these conversations take place?

What is the object which is being brought back?

What is B's attitude in dialogue 3? Can you explain this?

Some useful ways of expressing gratitude

(See unit 3.12)

Production

In pairs, try to write a continuation of either dialogue 2 or dialogue 3.

It occasionally happens that we damage things we borrow. Try to find a situation like this through group discussion. Then, in pairs, write out a short dialogue where one person is thanking the other and trying tactfully to mention the damage. Compare your version with others.

3.14 I'm so sorry
(Sympathy)

1   A: *No, they didn't even tell him – just sent a note.*
    B: *After fourteen years!*
    A: *Fifteen in May – if he'd stayed on.*
    B: *Oh, that's terrible. I'm so sorry.*
    A: *And of course at his age nobody wants to look at him.*
    B: *I am sorry . . . Poor Joss.*

2   A: *. . . and why was that, Mrs Naylor?*
    B: *They didn't give a real reason. Something about 'economy cuts' . . .*
    A: *I'm most distressed to hear about it . . .*
    B: *And only five years to go. I can't understand it.*
    A: *You have all my sympathy. And if there's anything I can do . . .*
    B: *That's very good of you . . . Oh, I still can't quite get over it.*

3   A: *But how could they!?*
    B: *I don't know myself, I really don't.*
    A: *Oh, my poor Joss . . .*
    B: *Five of us – all at the same time . . .*
    A: *It's terrible. I don't know how they have the nerve.*
    B: *Aye . . .*
    A: *Never mind, Joss. You'll find something else. Something better, maybe.*

4   A: *Sorry, I can't see her!*
    B: *She's been waiting all morning.*
    A: *Believe me, I am extremely sorry, but we had no choice.*
    B: *Couldn't you tell her yourself?*
    A: *What difference would it make? . . . Look, explain to her that we regret it as much as anyone else and that we'll do all we can to help them out.*

Interpretation

For each of the dialogues, say who you think the two speakers are and who the person is that they are talking about.
Where do you think each of the conversations is taking place?
What is the event which has upset everyone?
In which dialogue are the speakers most genuinely distressed? Put the dialogues in order, from most to least distressed.

Some useful ways of expressing sympathy

I'm sorry (to hear it).
I'm really terribly/very/extremely sorry.
I'm *so* sorry.
Oh how terrible/awful/upsetting/annoying/etc. . . .
Oh what a nuisance/disaster/business . . .
I can't tell you how sorry/upset I am.
I don't know what to say.

Production

For each dialogue, try to work out what must have been said immediately before the first line.

In pairs, choose one of the dialogues and try to make it longer. One of the people in the conversation should have a bright idea which changes the mood. Exchange versions with others.

Writing

Write a brief letter to a friend saying how sorry you are about a recent misfortune of his and offering some form of help.

Imagine that the dialogues are from a play. They come in this order: 3, 1, 2, 4. Write out the story of the play and give it an ending.

3.15 Oh yes I will
(Intention)

1 A: *What are you going to do?*
   B: *Tear it up.*
   A: *No, but seriously . . .*
   B: *I don't intend to do anything.*
   A: *But you can't just ignore it.*
   B: *Why not?*
   A: *Well . . .*
   B: *I'm not going to do anything about it.*

2 A: *Did you see this? . . .*
   B: *Uh-huh.*
   A: *Well?*
   B: *I refuse to have anything to do with it.*
   A: *But you can't.*
   B: *I will not be pushed around!*

3 A: *We should like to know what you propose to do.*
   B: *Nothing.*
   A: *Is this your final decision?*
   B: *It is.*
   A: *You have read this, I take it?*
   B: *We have . . . But we do not plan to change our scheme.*

Interpretation

In each of the dialogues decide who you think A and B are. Give their age, their position, their relationship to each other.
In which dialogues do the speakers know each other best? And least?
What do you think 'it' is in each of the dialogues?
In which of the dialogues are the speakers most hostile to each other?
In which dialogue is B most determined?
Where is each dialogue taking place?

Some useful ways of expressing intention

I'm (not) going to . . .
I (don't) intend to/-ing . . .
I've no intention of . . .-ing.
I'm thinking of/considering . . .-ing.
I've decided/made up my mind/resolved to . . .

My idea is to . . .
What I plan to do is . . .
This is/here's/what I intend to do . . .

Production

You are the boss of a small factory. One of your employees has found out that you have been cheating the income-tax authorities, but he has done nothing about it. You have fallen in love with this man's girl-friend, who also works for you. She seems to return the feeling you have for her. He comes to ask you for a largish loan so that he can get married. What do you intend to do? Discuss this problem in your group. When you have a solution, go to another group and compare it with theirs.

3.16 Now what?
(Asking about intention)

1 A: *And now what are you going to do?!*
 B: *Oh, shut up!*
 A: *I suppose I'm to blame?*
 B: *Look, just keep quiet and let me think.*
 A: *You'll have plenty of time for that. It doesn't seem as if we're going to get out of here in a hurry.*

2 A: *Where?*
 B: *Well, unfortunately we don't quite know.*
 A: *So, what do you plan to do?*
 B: *We thought we might see if you can find their tracks.*
 A: *And what do you think you're going to do if you find them?*
 B: *Follow them, of course.*
 A: *At this time of day?*

3 A: *I should like to know what measures you intend to take.*
 B: *I propose we call in the army.*
 A: *To do what exactly?*
 B: *Help search.*
 A: *Up here? I doubt if they'll be much help.*

4 A: *What shall we do, though?*
 B: *There isn't much we can do, except wait.*
 A: *But couldn't you phone them again?*
 B: *I phoned an hour ago. No news.*
 A: *Aren't you going to go down and see if you can help?*
 B: *There's no way I can help. I'd just be in the way.*

Interpretation

For each dialogue, say who you think the speakers are. Give their age, profession, importance, relationship to each other.
Where is each of the conversations taking place?
What exactly has happened?
Why is A so anxious to know B's intentions in each dialogue?

Some useful ways of asking about intention

What are you/we going to do about it?
What do you intend/plan to do about it?
What are you thinking of doing about it?
Aren't you going to do anything about it?
Don't you intend to do anything about it?
I'd like to know/could you tell me what you're going to do about it?

Production

Individually, note down a difficult situation you can remember yourself being in with a friend. Compare this with others in your group. What sort of questions did you ask each other about the ways of getting out of the situation?

3.17 If only ...
(Want or desire)

1 A: *God, I wish I could get out of this place!*
   B: *Well, why don't you do something about it, then?*
   A: *Like what?*
   B: *Take the paper and look at the ads.*
   A: *Waste of time. They're always taken before you get there.*

2 A: *Of course, we would like to find something a bit roomier.*
   B: *This doesn't look bad, though.*
   A: *No, I suppose it's all right. But it would be nice to have a spare room.*
   B: *Well, if you were prepared to move further north ...*
   A: *No, Geoffrey wants to stay here ...*

3 A: *It's the wallpaper, she says ... No, we can't. I'd love to, but the place isn't ours ... Well, basically, something brighter ... Oh, anywhere'll do ... Yes, we'd like to if we could ... Oh, I doubt it ... In ten years time, maybe.*

4 A: *I'd love to be able to, though. Just for a while.*
   B: *Wouldn't it be a bit lonely?*
   A: *Not necessarily ... I'd like to try, anyway.*
   B: *I couldn't stand it – not even for a week.*

Interpretation

Say who you think the speakers are in each dialogue.
Where do you think each of these conversations is taking place? Try
to describe the surroundings in detail.
In dialogue 4, what do you think the speakers have just been talking
about before the dialogue begins?
In which dialogue is B most aggressive?
In which dialogue is A most optimistic? And pessimistic?
What is the person on the other end of the line saying in dialogue 3?

Some useful ways of expressing want or desire

I wish I could . . .   Wouldn't it be nice/great/
I'd really like/love to . . .   marvellous to . . .?
If only I could . . .   Wouldn't it be nice if I could . . .
It would be (so) nice to . . .   That's (not) what I want.
I want to . . .

Production

In pairs, choose either dialogue 1 or dialogue 2 and try to continue it.
B must try to make A come to a positive decision. Now, write out
only B's words. Leave a space for A's replies. Pass the paper to
another pair. They must fill in A's words. Compare final results.

Write down individually three important changes you would really
like to make in your life. Take turns in saying these to the group as a
whole. The group should try to persuade you to realise your wishes
or ambitions.

3.18 Anyone for tennis?
(Asking about want or desire)

1 A: *Yes?*
B: *Do you mind if I come in?*
A: *Er . . . what's it about?*
B: *Well, if you could spare a few minutes . . .*
A: *Look, what do you want?*

2 A: *Fred!*
B: *Yeah.*
A: *Man here wants to see you!*
B: *Who is it?*
A: *Dunno.*
B: *What's he want?*
A: *What d'you want?*
C: *I want to speak to Fred.*
A: *Says he wants to speak to you.*

3 A: *Were you looking for something?*
B: *Well, yes . . . actually . . .*
A: *What was it you wanted?*
B: *Oh, it's nothing important. I'll just wait here, if that's all right.*
A: *Well, if there's nothing I can do for you . . .*
B: *Not for the moment, thanks.*

4 A: *Now what is it?*
B: *If you'll let me in, I'll explain.*
A: *You can explain here.*
B: *It won't take five minutes.*
A: *All right . . . Well, what is it?*

Interpretation

Close your eyes and try to see the people who are talking in each of the dialogues. What do they look like? What sort of clothes are they wearing? Are they old? Do they look well-off or poor? Are they doing a job? Do they know each other well? Do they look happy? Angry? Puzzled?

What exactly is it that the speaker wants in each dialogue? And *why* does he want it?

Try to visualise the physical surroundings for each dialogue.

In dialogue 3, why do you think B does not want to say what it is he wants?

Some useful ways of asking about want or desire

What do you want?
What is it (you want)?
Could you tell me what you want?
Is there anything you want/ need?
Is there anything I can do for you?

Can I do anything for you?
Can I help you?
Were you looking for something/someone?
Wouldn't you like ...?

Production

In pairs, decide what precisely the unexpected visitor wanted. Take five minutes, then present your suggestions to the class as a whole.

As a group, decide on one formal and one informal situation where you would need to ask someone what he wanted. Then work in pairs within the group to write very short dialogues (four lines) for each situation. Compare dialogues.

Part four:
Expressing and finding out about
moral attitudes

4.1 I didn't mean it
(Apologising)

1 A: *Good morning.*
  B: *Good morning.*
  A: *I've come to apologise.*
  B: *That's very good of you . . . er . . . What for?*
  A: *Last night.*
  B: *Last night?*
  A: *I believe you came to complain about the noise and I . . . was rather rude to you.*
  B: *Not to me. Must have been the guy next door. I didn't get in till half past four.*
  A: *Oh . . . Sorry to have got you out of bed then.*
  B: *It's all right.*

2 A: *Hey!*
  B: *Mmm?*
  A: *Sorry, if I woke you last night.*
  B: *Hmm?*
  A: *I said I'm sorry for waking you last night.*
  B: *Did you?*
  A: *You mean you didn't hear me?*
  B: *Not a thing.*
  A: *That's strange, 'cos I woke up screaming.*

3 A: *Yes?*
  B: *Please excuse me for disturbing you. I realise it's very early . . .*
  A: *Hm?*
  B: *I hope you enjoyed yourselves last night.*
  A: *Hm?*
  B: *It sounded very lively from underneath.*
  A: *Hm? Oh. Were we making a noise? Sorry.*
  B: *'A noise' is putting it mildly.*

4 A: *Philip Harvey here . . . Yes, that's right, just above you . . . I'd like to apologise for what seems to have happened on Saturday . . . No, no, I wasn't there – unfortunately . . . It was my son . . . He said what!?*

... *Oh, I'm extremely sorry* ... *No, I certainly will not* ... *Please accept my apologies – and my regards to your wife.*

5 A: *God you were making a din last night!*
   B: *Who? Me?*
   A: *The whole bloody lot of you.*
   B: *Why didn't you come and join us then?*
   A: *I told you, I had to get up early this morning.*
   B: *Well you did, didn't you?*
   A: *No thanks to you.*
   B: *O.K. I'm sorry.*
   A: *You sound it.*

Interpretation

What are the relationships between the people in each of the dialogues?

In which dialogue do they know each other best?

Try to form a picture of where each conversation is taking place.

What does B really mean in dialogue 3 when he says 'I hope you enjoyed yourselves last night'?

In dialogue 1, A says, 'I *believe* you came to complain' and in dialogue 4, A says 'for what *seems* to have happened'. What do the two words in italics tell you about the attitude of the speaker?

What is really meant by 'You sound it' in dialogue 5?

What is the other person saying in dialogue 4?

Some useful ways of apologising

I'm very/terribly/awfully/etc. sorry.
I'd like to apologise for...

Please forgive/excuse me for ...
I really must apologise for ...
Sorry about that.

Production

What sort of language do you need in order to apologise: a) if you know the person well? b) if he is a superior? c) if you do not like him very much? d) if he is very sensitive?

In pairs, invent an ending for dialogue 3 – A should try to counter-attack B. Then exchange solutions with others.

Writing

You forgot to keep an appointment. Decide who it was with, then write a brief note to apologise, suggesting another date and time.

4.2 How stupid of me!
(Apologising)

1 A: *Well, are you ready?*
   B: *I've been ready since two.*
   A: *Since ... Oh, was it two?*
   B: *Well, that's what you said.*
   A: *Oh, you must forgive me. It's been one hell of a day!*

2 A: *Ah,* there *you are. What happened?*
   B: *Nothing special ... Why?*
   A: *I couldn't imagine what had delayed you.*
   B: *Am I late?*
   A: *Well, we did say two o'clock.*
   B: *That's odd. I noted down three.*
   A: *That was what we first said, then you ...*
   B: *Quite so. I had forgotten. Please excuse me.*
   A: *It's quite all right.*

3 A: *I'm terribly late. I do apologise.*
   B: *Yes, I was beginning to wonder ...*
   A: *Just couldn't get away, I'm afraid. I hope you haven't been waiting long?*
   B: *Not too long.*
   A: *Good. Shall we go then?*

4 A: *Mr Barker?*
   B: *Yes, that's me.*
   A: *Do come in. You've had a bit of a wait, I'm afraid.*
   B: *Oh, it's all right.*
   A: *It was three o'clock you were supposed to see me, wasn't it?*
   B: *Two o'clock, actually.*
   A: *Good heavens! Have you been here since two? I* am *sorry.*
   B: *Oh, don't worry ...*

Interpretation

For each of the dialogues try to say who the speakers are and what their relationship is. Which pieces of language help you to work these things out?

What do you think the two people are going to do now that they have eventually met?

What do you think the reasons were for A's being late in each case?

In which dialogue do you think A is most sincere in his apologies? And least?

In which dialogue is the atmosphere most tense?

Where do you think A has just come from?

Some useful ways of apologising

(See unit 4.1)

Production

In pairs, decide on a situation which requires an apology from one person to another. It should be something fairly serious. Then work out a dialogue in which A attempts to apologise but B will not accept the apology. A is therefore driven to try to convince B of his sincerity. When you have finished, compare your dialogue with those of others.

4.3 Never mind
(Forgiving)

1 A: *When I was telling that joke about the alcoholic priest, I had no idea her husband . . .*
  B: *Don't worry. You couldn't have known.*
  A: *I really am sorry, though. I'm always doing this.*
  B: *Oh, it doesn't matter.*
  A: *It mucked up your dinner, though. I'm sorry.*
  B: *Never mind, Jeff, never mind.*

2 A: *Then he's a damn fool!*
  B: *My brother is not a damn fool!*
  A: *Well, why should he object to being called Charlie, then?*
  B: *Because his name is Charles.*
  A: *If he's that fussy about it, he should stick out his hand and say 'I'm Charles, not Charlie. Pleased to meet you . . .'*
  B: *You've still no right to call him a damn fool.*
  A: *All right, I'm sorry. I wasn't thinking.*
  B: *I'm sorry, too. You're right, really – he is rather pompous.*

3 A: *You'll have to excuse me, I seem to have offended one of your colleagues.*
  B: *Oh, Philipson, I shouldn't worry about that.*
  A: *He seemed very annoyed. I don't know why.*
  B: *It's his title. He's very touchy about it. You referred to him as Sales Manager.*
  A: *And what is he?*
  B: *Marketing Manager!*
  A: *Oh, I see. Well, tell him I'm extremely sorry!*
  B: *All right, I will.*

4 A: *Please forgive me. I had no idea . . .*
  B: *It doesn't matter.*
  A: *If only I'd known.*
  B: *It's quite all right.*
  A: *Believe me, I . . .*
  B: *It's quite all right, I said.*

Interpretation

Who is talking to whom in each of these dialogues?
What is the reason for the apology in each dialogue?
Where exactly is each conversation taking place?
In which dialogue is the atmosphere most relaxed? And most tense?
If you had to apologise about something, which of these people
would you prefer to do it to?

Some useful ways of forgiving

O.K.
All right.
(Please) Don't worry (about it).
Never mind.
Forget it.
It wasn't your fault.
It was nobody's fault.

You couldn't help it/have done
anything about it.
There was nothing you could
have done.
I don't want you to feel bad
about it.

Production

In each case, one of the speakers has 'put his foot in it'. How does he
get out of it? In pairs, work out convincing excuses for each dialogue
in no more than four sentences.

Have you ever made a 'gaffe' or dropped a clanger, i.e. said
something which, without your knowing it, was very embarrassing
to someone else present? Share your experiences with the others in
your group. Then work out acceptable ways of apologising in that
situation.

4.4 Well done!
(Approval)

1 A: *So I said 'If you're not prepared to pay for the paper, I'm not going to do it!'*

B: *Quite right . . . And what did he say?*

A: *Oh, something about it not being his job.*

B: *Well, if it's not his job why did he ask you to do it?*

A: *Exactly!*

2 A: *However, I pointed out that we could not be expected to pay for the paper.*

B: *I'm glad you did.*

A: *I also told him that he would be held responsible for any delay.*

B: *Excellent.*

3 A: *Look, you can't expect us to pay for the paper as well.*

B: *But I entirely agree.*

A: *Oh . . . Well, I suggest that the company pays.*

B: *Good idea.*

A: *You have no objections?*

B: *None at all. I'm delighted with the whole scheme.*

Interpretation

Try to describe the appearance of the speakers in each of the dialogues, basing your opinion on the way they sound and what they say.

What do you think the 'paper' is going to be used for?

Say exactly where each conversation is happening.

In which of the dialogues is there a surprising reaction?

How would you describe A's attitude in dialogue 2? And in dialogue 3?

Some useful ways of expressing approval

(Quite) Right.

Very good (indeed).

Good idea/thing/for you.

Absolutely.

Great/excellent/splendid/fine.

Well done.

I'm very pleased with/happy about/glad that . . .

That was fine/excellent/magnificent/etc.

What you did/said was excellent/just right/fine/etc.

Production

Someone has just come to tell you that he has done something for you which he is sure will please you. In pairs, decide on what this might be. Then work out short exchanges to show how you would express your approval, a) to a much younger person, b) to a much older person, c) to an inferior, d) to a superior, e) to someone you like a lot, f) to someone you do not like very much.

4.5 It won't do
(Disapproval)

1 A: *But why did you take it?*
    B: *I couldn't say no.*
    A: *Why not?*
    B: *He'd have been offended.*
    A: *Too bad. You still shouldn't have taken it.*

2 A: *. . . and what are we supposed to do with this?*
    B: *Couldn't it be . . . sent back?*
    A: *That's not the sort of thing you can just send back . . .*
    B: *Perhaps we could offer to pay for it.*
    A: *No, I really don't think you should've accepted it in the first place.*
    B: *It was very difficult to refuse.*
    A: *Yes, but you ought to have known better.*

3 A: *I still don't approve of it.*
    B: *But why not? What's wrong with taking it?*
    A: *You never know . . .*
    B: *Oh, you're so suspicious.*
    A: *Perhaps I am, but I still think you shouldn't have taken it.*

4 A: *It's a pity you didn't tell me first.*
    B: *But I didn't know . . .*
    A: *Like hell you didn't!*
    B: *I didn't think there was anything in it.*
    A: *That's just why he gave it to you.*
    B: *But I didn't know . . .*
    A: *All right, all right – it's just a pity you didn't come to me first, that's all.*

Interpretation

Try to decide why one of the speakers feels entitled to criticise the other. Is it because he is older, in a superior position, more domineering as a character, etc.?

Can you visualise the surroundings in each of the dialogues?

What is the thing which should not have been accepted?

Why is one speaker criticising the other?

What does A mean in dialogue 4 when he says, 'Like hell you didn't!'?

In which dialogue is the atmosphere most strained? And most relaxed?

Some useful ways of expressing disapproval

You shouldn't have ...

Why (on earth) did you ...?

It's a pity/shame/unfortunate you ... (didn't) ...

It would've been better if you ...

I don't approve/I strongly disapprove.

I can't say I approve.

I'm afraid I didn't like that.

That was wrong of you/him etc.

I wish you hadn't ...

Production

In pairs, extend one of the dialogues. Try to decide what should be done with 'it'. Write out your dialogue and discuss it with others.

We have all done things we knew were 'wrong'. And other people are always quick to disapprove. Write down, individually, one such personal experience. Exchange these written versions. Now, each person should tell the group about the 'wrong' act on his slip of paper. Allow for discussion.

4.6 Interesting...
(Appreciation or reservation)

1 A: *How are you enjoying it?*
 B: *Oh, it's excellent. Very good, indeed. Don't you think?*
 A: *Not bad at all, considering . . .*
 B: *Yes, when you think how little time they had . . .*

2 A: *Well, what do you think?*
 B: *Remarkable, isn't it!*
 A: *Do you think so?*
 B: *Oh, for amateurs, I mean.*

3 A: *You're enjoying yourselves, I'm sure.*
 B: *Yes – thank you.*
 A: . *They're very good, aren't they!*
 C: *Yes.*
 B: *Yes.*
 A: *So full of life!*
 B: *Yes, they're very lively, I must say.*
 A: *I suppose you've never seen anything like this before.*
 C: *Not quite like this, no . . .*

4 A: *Good, isn't it?*
 B: *I've seen worse.*
 A: *You don't like it?*
 B: *No, it's O.K.*

5 A: *I'm sorry I wasn't able to be with you.*
 B: *That's . . . that's all right.*
 A: *And how was it?*
 B: *Very pleasant, thank you.*
 A: *You didn't find it too long?*
 B: *Well, it could have been a bit shorter . . .*

Interpretation

What are the relationships between the speakers in each of the dialogues? How long do you think they have known each other? Put the dialogues in order, starting with the longest acquaintanceship and ending with the shortest.
What is the object or event to which each dialogue refers?
Where exactly is each conversation happening?
What exactly does A mean in dialogue 2 when he says, 'Do you think so'?
How would you describe B's reaction in dialogue 4?
What do you think C is trying to *avoid* saying by using the words 'Not quite like this, no . . .' in dialogue 3?
In which of the dialogues do the speakers *really* share the same opinion?

Some useful ways of expressing appreciation or reservations

It's very nice/pleasant/interesting/beautiful/striking/etc.
I (*do*) like that.
It was excellent/very good/most impressive/delightful/etc.
Wonderful! Marvellous! Great!

Not bad, but . . .
I think it's a bit loud/bright/short/sweet/etc.
Interesting . . .
It'll do for a start.
I think it would've been better if . . .

Production

Try to extend two of the conversations. The next speaker will start by saying 'What do you mean?' Write down your extended version and exchange it with someone else. He should decide which dialogues you had in mind.

Write down individually three things you have seen or experienced recently that you are really enthusiastic about. Then take it in turns to tell the rest of the group what each thing was and how you felt about it. Anyone can stop you and disagree with you.

Writing

Write a *very brief* review of a book you have read, or a film or play you have seen recently and which you liked. Show your appreciation but express reservations where appropriate.

4.7   I wish I'd . . .
(Regret)

1   A: *Yes, I have.*
    B: *And?*
    A: *I doubt if we'll be able to use it.*
    B: *What was wrong with it?*
    A: *Basically: too much desert and too much commentary. It's too long.*
    B: *Couldn't I cut it?*
    A: *Too late, I'm afraid. Pity you didn't think of that before.*

2   A: *Well, if you want my opinion, the answer's no . . . Why? It's too
scrappy . . . confused . . . too much desert and too little commentary . . .
Hm? . . . I don't care whose son he is . . . I'm sorry, Bert, but it just
isn't good enough . . . That's just too bad . . . I know, but it's tough
for everyone . . . Well, it might help a bit, but . . .*

3   A: *No, I didn't say that!*
    B: *But you don't like it?*
    A: *Look, that's not what I said . . . I said I thought it was a pity . . . er
. . . I thought it was a pity you set it in the desert. That's all.*
    B: *But I don't understand . . .*
    A: *It was too . . . um . . . I don't want to say flat . . . er . . . you know
what I mean? I mean, if only you'd had a bit more variety . . .*
    B: *Like?*
    A: *Well, I don't know . . . I mean, a bit less of the desert stuff.*

4   A: *So, nobody wants to take it?*
    B: *No.*
    A: *What a pity you didn't see me before you went.*
    B: *I tried, but you weren't here . . . But they all say different things: it's
too long, it's too short, too much desert, not enough . . .*
    A: *I know . . . I'm sorry about that . . . I could have warned you they
wouldn't take it . . .*
    B: *Pity you didn't!*

Interpretation

Who are the speakers in each of the dialogues? Give their age, occupation, status, relationship to each other, etc.
Where is each conversation taking place?
What are they talking about in each dialogue?
In which dialogue is the speaker most helpful? And least?
Which of these 'refusers' would you prefer to have to deal with? Why?

Some useful ways of expressing regret

It's a pity
What a pity $\Big\}$ you didn't . . .
I'm very sorry, but I'm afraid . . .
If only I had . . .
There's nothing I can do, I'm afraid.
Nobody regrets this more than I do, but . . .
I greatly regret having to/that I shall have to/that it will be necessary to . . .

Production

With the others in your group, discuss the remarks which might have led up to each of the dialogues.

Imagine that someone has just made you a proposition. Decide what the proposition is and work out three objections to it. Now write your proposition on a slip of paper and pass it to another member of the group. Group members now take it in turns to make the propositions they have been given. The others should make objections and appropriate expressions of regret.

Writing

You are a businessman. Someone has written to you making a proposal. Decide what the proposal is, then write a polite letter regretting that you cannot accept it, and giving reasons.

4.8 So what?
(Indifference)

1 A: *So, first we'll go to the museum, all right?*
    B: *If you like.*
    A: *And that's next to the Cathedral, so we could get the Cathedral in before lunch. How does that suit you?*
    B: *I'm easy.*
    A: *Then in the afternoon . . . How about the Fortress?*
    B: *O.K.*

2 A: *They want to know what you'd like to do in the morning.*
    B: *Oh – anything.*
    A: *Would the museum be all right?*
    B: *I suppose so.*
    A: *Then, after that, would you prefer to have lunch or see the Cathedral?*
    B: *I don't care, quite honestly. Just leave it to them.*

3 A: *What are we going to do with them?*
    B: *Take them to the Museum, I suppose.*
    A: *I suppose so . . . Then?*
    B: *Well, there's the Cathedral.*
    A: *All right.*
    B: *And that's half the day.*
    A: *They'll probably want to see the Fortress, too. What d'you think?*
    B: *It's all the same to me – I'm sick of the whole thing.*

Interpretation

Try to imagine what the speakers look like in each dialogue.
How well do they know each other?
What exactly is the situation in each dialogue?
Why are these visits being proposed?
Where is the town in which the museum and the cathedral are situated?
In which dialogue is A most enthusiastic? And least enthusiastic?
In dialogue 3, who do you think 'they' are?

Some useful ways of expressing indifference

If you like.
(Do) as you like.
I suppose so.
I don't mind/care.
Who cares?
So what?
Why not?

Too bad.
I'm easy.
It's all the same to me.
It doesn't matter (to me).
It makes no difference (to me/
either way).

Production

We often find ourselves in circumstances where other people offer us a number of things, none of which we really want to do or accept, but which we feel we cannot refuse. With the others in your group, try to remember some personal experiences of this kind. How do you react to such proposals? How do you show that you do not care one way or the other?

Part five:
Getting things done

5.1 Why don't we . . .?
(Making suggestions)

1 A: *Why don't we put it in orange juice bottles?*
B: *What the hell for!*
A: *Well, then they'll think it's orange juice.*
B: *It isn't the same colour.*
A: *Mmm – true . . . Then, d'you know what – let's put it in old wine bottles.*
B: *We'd still have to pay for the wine.*
A: *Mmm . . . what about the radiator?*
B: *And have it boil over!*

2 A: *Look, there's no problem. You put three in your rucksack and we'll stuff the rest into the cot.*
B: *But they're sure to look at me. I was stripped coming in.*
C: *And I'm not putting that stuff in with the baby.*
A: *All right, all right. Look, you hold the baby. We'll dump it into the cot and he can put his rucksack on top.*
B: *And if they find it?*
C: *I don't know why we have to go to all this trouble.*
A: *If they find it, they find it. Too bad.*

3 A: *I have a better suggestion. Why doesn't one of us take it all?*
B: *And if they stop him?*
A: *It's a risk we have to take. And, anyway, if they find it on one of us they're sure to search the rest.*
B: *And who's going to carry all that?*
A: *Well, if nobody else wants to . . .*

Interpretation

Who are A, B (and C)? How well do they know each other?
Where do you think they are? How did they get there? Where are
they going – if anywhere?
What do you think 'it' is in each dialogue?
Who is 'they' in each dialogue?
What is the attitude of A and B to 'they'?

Some useful ways of making suggestions

Let's . . .   How (what) about . . .-ing.
I suggest we . . .   We might try . . .-ing.
Why don't we . . .   I suggest . . .-ing.
Couldn't we . . .
I propose (that) we . . .

Production

Decide who the characters in each dialogue are and what their
predicament is. Then write down, in no more than ten lines, what
you think they are going to do. This exercise should take no more
than ten minutes. When you have finished, exchange your solutions
with others in the group. Compare and discuss.

5.2 Let's...
(Making suggestions)

1   A: *Why don't we put them up in the Underground?*
      B: *They'd never let us.*
      A: *But if we don't ask ...*
      B: *How d'you mean?*
      A: *Each of us could take a few. Put them up quickly, and jump on a train.*

2   A: *We could always hand them out in the streets, I suppose ...*
      B: *You and who else?*
      A: *Well, I thought ... Or, how about putting a few small ads in the papers?*
      B: *D'you know how much that costs?*
      A: *Well, we might shorten it a bit ...*
      B: *No, no – you've got to think big. Posters, banners, placards, that sort of thing ...*

3   A: *I suggest we start with the larger towns in the Midlands – do you agree? – take all available space for a week – right? – back this up with regular spots on radio and TV – O.K.? – Then I propose we launch a special 'week in the country' programme, get right out into the villages. We could also have a try-out in the south, in Bristol for instance. Now, I'd like you to ...*

Interpretation

How old do you think the speakers are in each of the dialogues? Do you think this affects what they say and how they say it?

Try to imagine what jobs these people are involved in doing.

Close your eyes and try to see the surroundings in which each of the dialogues takes place. Is it a room? Are the people standing or sitting?

What objects are there nearby?

In which dialogues is there an optimist and in which a pessimist?

What is the subject of each of the dialogues?

How would you describe B's attitude in dialogue 2?

Some useful ways of making suggestions

Let's . . .   How (what) about . . .-ing?
I suggest we . . .   We might try . . .-ing.
Why don't we . . .?   I suggest . . .-ing.
Couldn't we . . .?
I propose we . . .

Production

In pairs, try to write a continuation of dialogue 1 or dialogue 2 – A always suggests and B always objects. Then compare it with another pair's work

Imagine you are organising a party for the whole class. Split into three equal groups; each group should make detailed plans for the party. Specify the following: invitations – any outsiders? food and drink – what kind and how much? place? time? music? Each group should then present its proposal to the whole class. Objections may be raised.

5.3 Could you possibly?
(Asking for assistance)

1 A: *Could you do me a favour?*
 B: *Sure.*
 A: *I need someone to sign this for me.*
 B: *This!*
 A: *All you have to do is say it's a true likeness of me, and sign your name.*
 B: *O.K.*

2 A: *Good morning, do you mind if I come in for a moment, thank you, we're from your district and we're collecting signatures for the anti-AFY movement, and we only need 573 more, so if we could have yours, all of yours in fact, we'd be very grateful, if you wouldn't mind signing here ... and here ... and once again, here, thank you very much for your support, goodbye ...*

3 A: *Now if we could just have a little signature here ... Thank you ... and here.*
 B: *Just a minute. What's this?*
 A: *Oh, that's just the procedure in case of non-payment ...*
 B: *Ah.*
 A: *That's right. And now, would you be so kind as to sign just once more ... here ... and ... here. Thank you very very much ...*

4 A: *I understand, but until we have your signature nothing can be done.*
 B: *All we are waiting for is the surveyor's estimate.*
 A: *I guarantee you'll have it by tomorrow ... Would you mind, then, signing now so that we can send the papers off today.*
 B: *It's somewhat irregular ...*
 A: *We'd be very grateful if you could*

Interpretation

For each dialogue say who the people are. Give their age, occupation, status, relationship to each other, etc.
What is being signed in each case?
Where is each conversation taking place?
What kind of people is A talking to in 2?
How would you describe B's attitude in dialogue 3? and 4?
What is A trying to do in dialogue 3? Notice his use of 'little' and 'just'.

Some useful ways of asking for assistance

Can/could you . . . for me?
I'd be most (very) grateful if you could . . .
You couldn't . . . could you?
Could you possibly . . .?
Would you mind . . .-ing?
I want to . . .

You don't mind . . .-ing, do you?
Kindly . . .
If you don't mind, I'd like you to . . .
Please . . . will/would you?

Production

In pairs, discuss how one of the dialogues might continue if B suddenly begins to raise objections *after* he has signed. When your dialogue is ready, compare it with others.

5.4 Do come
(Making invitations)

1 A: *Why don't you join us, then?*
  B: *Mmm ... How are you going?*
  A: *There are four of us already. We need a fifth.*
  B: *Yes, but how are you going?*
  A: *By minibus.*
  B: *Ah-hah ... Mind if I think it over?*
  A: *Well, don't take too long.*

2 A: *D'you remember ... ? ... Yes, almost a year ago ... that's right ...*
  Anyway, you got the letter? Good ... Uh-huh ... Well, we were
  wondering if you would care to join us ... Yes, yes, it is rather ...
  No, I don't think so ... Oh, do come if you can ... Thursday at the
  latest ... Hm? Oh, by minibus ... Oh, I see. Yes, that might be a
  problem ...

3 A: *How about it, then?*
  B: *No go.*
  A: *Oh, come on ...*
  B: *Sorry.*
  A: *It's free ...*
  B: *Only because you need a driver.*

4 A: *... and we're going with them.*
  B: *Oh, I envy you!*
  A: *Well, wouldn't you like to join us, then?*
  B: *Why not?*
  A: *Good. Then I'll let them know ... You can drive, can't you?*
  B: *It depends what.*
  A: *A minibus.*
  B: *Oh, you're going by minibus!*

Interpretation

What do you think the relationship is between the speakers in each dialogue?
Where is each conversation taking place?
Why do you think B is being invited in each case?
Do you think B will agree to go?
Where are A and his friends planning to go and for what reason?
What is the other person saying to A in dialogue 2?

Some useful ways of making invitations

How/what about . . .?
How would you like to . . .?
Would/wouldn't you like to . . .?
I'd like you to . . .

Perhaps you'd like/care to . . .
Would you be interested in . . .?
I'd like to invite you to/for . . .
I propose . . .-ing
May I suggest . . .-ing?

Production

Write down on a piece of paper your name and two things you do not enjoy but which many other people might find enjoyable (e.g. watching a football match, travelling by sea, etc.). Put all the slips into a box. Then take turns in drawing a slip. Talk to the person whose name is on the slip and invite him to do one of the things he has written. He should try to avoid accepting.

Writing

Write a brief note to a friend inviting him or her to spend the weekend with you. You have a special reason for inviting your friend.

5.5 Not if I were you
(Giving advice)

1 A: *I think you ought to report it to the police.*
     B: *If I do, they'll want to know where I found it.*
     A: *Can't you tell them?*
     B: *They might want to know what I was doing there.*

2 A: *I reckon you'd better go to the police.*
     B: *Why?*
     A: *They're sure to notice it.*
     B: *So? They still don't know who's found it.*
     A: *As you like. I'd still go if I were you.*

3 A: *This ought to be reported to the police, don't you think?*
     B: *No, no, no – don't go to the police here.*
     A: *Why not?*
     B: *Nobody goes to the police unless he's taken.*
     A: *But I ... I ... can't possibly keep it.*
     B: *You know what I suggest? ... Don't say anything about it to anyone.*

Interpretation

Who are the speakers in each dialogue? Give age, occupation, relationship to each other, etc.
What has been found?
Where are the conversations happening?
What do you think the person who has found 'it' will do in each case?
How would you describe the attitude of the finder in each dialogue?

Some useful ways of giving advice

If I were you, I'd . . .
I think you'd better (not) . . .
(I think) you ought to . . .
(I think) you should . . .
(I think) it would be best if . . .

My advice to you is/would be . . .
If you take my advice, you'll . . .
I advise you (strongly) to . . .

Production

A set of pictures will be needed in each of which some action needs to be taken (e.g. a man in a suit too small for him). The pictures should be placed face downwards in the middle of the group. In pairs, take a picture. One person has to become the character in the picture, the other should offer him advice. He may find reasons for not accepting it.

5.6 Take it from me

(Giving advice)

1 A: *You ought to have it looked at.*
   B: *It's all right. It doesn't hurt.*
   A: *It looks nasty to me. Why don't you go?*
   B: *I'll see what it's like tomorrow.*

2 A: *Don't you think it would be better to have it examined?*
   B: *No. I trust my own judgement.*
   A: *Of course. But is it worth the risk? I do think you should ask for it to be examined.*
   B: *I'll think it over.*

3 A: *That looks very nasty. Very nasty.*
   B: *Oh . . .*
   A: *I think you'd better have it out.*
   B: *Oh no, I couldn't. I couldn't bear that.*
   A: *I wouldn't advise you to wait any longer.*
   B: *Just a month. Maybe it'll clear up.*
   A: *I can't force you, obviously, if you are against it. But I still recommend an operation . . .*

4 A: *You're the only one who can persuade him . . . I have tried, he won't listen to me . . . You've got to make him come round to it himself. If he thinks it's his idea, he'll do it . . . I know it's hard . . . Try telling him the truth, that may shock him out of it . . .*

Interpretation

Who are the speakers in each dialogue?
Do they know each other well?
What is 'it' in each dialogue?
Where are the conversations taking place?
How would you describe B's attitude in dialogue 1, 2 and 3?
What do you think B will decide to do in each case?
In which dialogue does A have the most right to offer advice?
What is the other person saying to A in dialogue 4?

Some useful ways of giving advice

(See unit 5.7)

Production

In pairs, work out a continuation of one of the dialogues. A should continue to try to persuade B, who should go on resisting. Compare your work with what others have done.

5.7 **Better not**
(Warning)

1 A: *Hitching!*
    B: *Uh-huh.*
    A: *You must be crazy!*
    B: *It's not so far.*
    A: *But alone! I wouldn't do it alone.*
    B: *I'll get there.*

2 A: *I don't approve.*
    B: *Why not?*
    A: *You've heard my reasons.*
    B: *But I'm not going alone now.*
    A: *I am still against it.*
    B: *You're against everything I do.*
    A: *Not quite everything . . .*

3 A: *What do you think?*
    B: *Sounds interesting. You've done it before, have you?*
    A: *No, this is the first time.*
    B: *Really? Don't you think you're taking a risk?*
    A: *Maybe . . . Are you against it?*
    B: *Well, let's say I'm not entirely in favour of it.*

4 A: *Now you've been warned . . .*
    B: *All right.*
    A: *If you go, we cannot be responsible for you.*
    B: *I know.*
    A: *Quite honestly – and if you'll excuse my saying so – I think you're making a mistake.*
    B: *We've been told that every time we've gone!*

Interpretation

Try to work out exactly who the people are in each of the dialogues. Close your eyes and try to imagine them: their age, their attitudes to one another, their clothing, etc.
What exactly is the thing that one of the speakers intends to do and which the other disapproves of?
Where is each conversation taking place?
Why in dialogue 2 does B say, 'But I'm *not* going alone now'?

Some useful ways of warning

I wouldn't (do that) if I were you.
You must be mad/crazy/ out of your mind.
I don't think that's very wise/advisable.
I think you're making a mistake.
I should be careful, if I were you.
It doesn't sound like a very good idea to me.
Rather you than me.
Well, go ahead if you must, but . . .

Production

In pairs, decide what was said immediately before each dialogue. Try to continue one of the dialogues. Compare your work with others in the group.

Individually, write on a slip of paper something dangerous or unusual you intend to do. Put the slips in a box. Then take turns in drawing one and saying what is written on it, e.g. 'I'm thinking of giving up my job and joining a commune.' The others in the group should express their doubts.

5.8 Keep off the grass!
(Instructing)

1 A: *Hey, Gus!*
  B: *What?*
  A: *Turn that down!*
  B: *What?*
  A: *Turn it down!*
  B: *Why?*
  A: *The Skinners'll start banging again.*
  B: *Oh, hell! O.K.*

2 A: *Excuse me.*
  B: *Uh-huh?*
  A: *Is anyone listening to this?*
  B: *Dunno.*
  A: *Well, do you think it could be turned down?*

3 A: *I realise, but it is Friday night.*
  B: *But it was the same last night. And the night before.*
  A: *I understand, but I don't think there's much I could do about it.*
  B: *I suggest you ask them to go somewhere else.*
  A: *It's not all that easy, you know.*

4 A: *You heard!*
  B: *What?*
  A: *I said 'switch it off!'*
  B: *Oh, yeah?*
  A: *Now don't you start getting cocky with me!*
  C: *Who the hell d'you think you are, hey?*
  A: *You turn that thing off right now or I'll . . .*
  B: *Or you'll? . . .*
  A: You heard!

Interpretation

What is the relationship between the people in each dialogue?
Where does each dialogue take place?
Who do you think 'they' are in dialogue 3?

Some useful ways of instructing

Stop that!
Don't do that!
You'd better not do that (again).

Get on with it.
Come on then/now.
What are you/we waiting for?
You'd better . . .

Production

Write down individually on separate slips of paper three things that other people do which annoy you. Put the slips in a box. Take turns to draw a slip and to address anyone else in the group, asking them to stop doing what is written on the slip, e.g. 'Please stop yawning'. The person addressed has to find an immediate response, e.g. 'Sorry, but I was up late last night . . .'

Appendix:
Possible interpretations of the dialogues

Unit 1.1
- Two businessmen waiting at an airport for a man they have not met (who is rather exotically dressed).
- Two ladies at a party discussing a celebrity.
- Two men who have suddenly spotted a man they know in a crowd, a man they thought was elsewhere . . . (his twin brother?)
- Two men planning a murder.
- Two people plotting an exchange of weapons/drugs/stolen goods.
- Two policemen searching for a missing person.
- A rich couple on an ocean liner who suddenly see a man who had been threatening them at home the week before.

Unit 1.2
- Two mountain-climbers returning from a long hike, arguing about the right way home.
- A husband and wife showing slides of their holiday (in Ireland); they disagree about the place they spent the night at.
- A hitch-hiker heading for a small village, being given a lift by an older man who thinks he knows the way better.
- A (young?) couple arguing in their car about the way to get to a friend's house for a party.
- Two people trying to find their way back (to a friend's? to the hotel?) at night in an unfamiliar town.
- Two hunters arguing about where they left their bags.

Unit 1.3
- Two people in a train, one of whom travels frequently on this line; the other is anxious to arrive . . .
- A nervous husband about to leave on a long journey; last time he went away he was late because his wife got the departure time wrong.
- A man in a travel bureau talking to an assistant (who has already given him the information twice).
- Timid secretary to overbearing boss; the secretary is in fact sure that the visitor they are expecting will arrive on the afternoon plane; she wants to check on the files . . .

Unit 1.4

- A man, who is always trying to get his married friends to go out drinking/ gambling/racing with him, rings up to arrange the next 'outing'. The wife answers the phone.
- The daughter has run away from home to share a flat with a friend in London. The angry father is trying to find out from his daughter's flatmate where she is.
- A secretary has been given strict instructions by her boss not to let a tiresome commercial traveller in to see him. She can use any excuse to keep him away. The secretary is being 'unhelpful'.
- The 'black sheep of the family' is hoping to borrow money from his hard-working brother. When he knocks at the door of his brother's flat, a woman he has never met before comes to the door. He is confused, and, not knowing what to do asks if he can leave a note.
- A man from the local 'Save our village church' fund-raising scheme was told by a rich businessman at a party to come round during the week and collect a donation. This is the fourth time he has called.

Unit 1.5

- A businessman in a hurry to a newspaper seller outside the tube.
- Mother to teenage son or daughter, who is still in bed on a Sunday morning.
- A half-drunk customer to a tired waiter who wants to close his café.
- A dentist to his assistant on a busy day.
- Two close friends who meet by chance in the street after not seeing each other for two years (one is hurrying to catch a train).
- A sports instructor taking a group of young children for a hike in the mountains.
- Guests, who have been trying to find a good excuse to leave.
- Two passengers on a jet flight, who have lost several hours, or, two people travelling by car in summer who cross from one time zone to another.

Unit 1.6

- A couple watching a TV film; one of the characters has a special glass cutter with him, yet smashes a shop window.
- A diabetic is found slumped over the wheel of his car; he has not taken his injection and his syringe is not in his pocket.
- A young couple are about to go out for the evening; they have just slammed the door of their flat, and are checking for the key . . .
- A deaf man (who has a hearing aid) has mysteriously disappeared; a detective is interviewing his wife.
- A large warehouse has been broken into; the guard, who has recently been put onto night service, has been discovered badly beaten up although he was armed.

Unit 2.1

– A recently married couple trying to give a party for some close friends; the husband suggests the friends should all bring something to eat and drink.

– Two of the organisers of a Congress (e.g. of technical translators), which is proving expensive to arrange; neither A nor B really likes the idea of asking people to pay ...

– The organisers of a cross-country run have been given a supply of T-shirts by an advertising agency to distribute to all the runners; one of the speakers feels that the runners should pay to take part in the race.

– A youth club arranged for its members to go and visit old people; one of the organisers thinks that the young people should have all their transport expenses paid, the other disagrees.

Unit 2.2

– A timid couple living in a rented flat have been asked by the landlord to pay for damage done by the last tenant.

– A man has just received a bill telling him to pay for a new fan-belt put into his car while it was being serviced at the garage; he is talking to another car-owner.

– An elderly woman has just come out of hospital; she finds she has been charged not only for the operation but for 'skin cure' as well; she is complaining to a friend over coffee.

– A couple have been buying clothes through a postal service scheme; during the past few weeks they have received several things they had not ordered but decided to pay for nevertheless; this time, however ...

– At the monthly board meeting of a company the manager explains that a container firm, which arranged delivery of their goods, had been charging for storage as well ...

Unit 2.3

– A young man and woman have decided to get married against her father's wishes ...

– A brother and sister have just learnt from the doctor that their father is seriously ill, and is likely to die ...

– A company has decided to sack some of its workers, particularly one, who is extremely troublesome; one of the directors feels it would be fair to warn this man, but the other ...

– Two women are discussing the daughter of a friend; the girl has been making money as a night-club 'hostess'; the two women feel that their friend ought to be told.

– A young couple, living in a very small flat, have had a 'friend' staying for over four weeks; they decide he must be asked to go, but one of them still hopes he may go of his own accord.

Unit 2.4

- Brother and sister: he has just bought a pure cotton shirt and has asked his sister how it should be washed ...
- A man complaining to the shop where he has recently bought a special kind of shelving made of different coloured woods; before fixing them to the wall he had been advised to ...
- The gardener of a large estate is complaining about his grass to the owner (both are rather stubborn people).
- A cheeky student nurse to one of her trainers; the student nurse has ruined the dinner of a patient on a special diet, or, has broken a delicate instrument (a thermometer?).
- A small photographic agency, where the owner has two not very polite assistants; a batch of photographs has been ruined because ...

Unit 2.5

- A and B are in a pub; A is a woman and is tired of always having her drinks paid for; on the other hand, the man she is with knows that she doesn't have much money.
- A and C have been staying for several days as the guests of B and D; they are having a farewell dinner together in a restaurant; A and C make a polite, but not too convincing, offer to pay the bill.
- B is older than A, but they have been friends for a long time; it was A's suggestion that they meet for lunch ...
- Two friends are queuing for theatre tickets; one of them tries to pay, because he knows his friend does not have much money, but the other will not let him ...
- Two people who have met for the first time (on a boat? a train? in a hotel? at a conference?) are eating together; one of them offers to pay, and insists on doing so.

Unit 2.6

- A man who does cookery demonstrations on television invites his neighbour (a man who has no interest in cooking) to come and watch him live in the studio.
- A husband and wife have been invited together to see an experimental play produced by the wife's brother-in-law; neither is particularly interested in the theatre ...
- An extremely energetic woman has almost persuaded one of her colleagues to take up yoga; the first session is on Friday ... (it might also be karate or modern dance).
- The editor of a Psychiatric Journal has been invited to attend a lecture by a person whose ideas he has little respect for ...
- The friend of a friend invites A to hear him give a talk on Oriental Religions; A has already heard this talk once, but he is not sure if the other person realises this ...

Unit 2.7

- Two English tourists in Wales have turned up a small country road; the farmer (?) is shouting at them, and at that moment someone else appears . .
- Two young travellers have reached a border crossing; they are carrying expensive cameras which were, in fact, bought in the country they are about to visit; they are trying to explain this to the border guard.
- An assistant film producer is trying to get a young actor to walk as if he had an artificial leg; the actor fails to see the point; finally the producer himself appears . . .
- A teacher of Spanish from England is in Spain; he is trying to explain something to a garage mechanic; a bystander mistakenly offers to help him.

Unit 2.8

- A has rented a TV set; the picture jumps; B, who is very proud of his skill with machines, offers to fix it.
- A has just bought an electric typewriter; his brother (whom he likes but does not have much faith in) offers to find out why it is not working properly.
- A has some complicated forms (tax? insurance?) to fill out and has been complaining to B about how difficult they are to fill out; B, an old friend, offers to help.
- B is an amateur mechanic, who fixes everything at home, and a neighbour of A's; A is having trouble with his second-hand car; B offers to fix it, but A . . .

Unit 2.9

- A secretary has been asked to contact somebody who has been invited to attend an important meeting; she has remembered to contact him, but . . .
- A long-lost relative has suddenly reappeared; he is extremely difficult to contact; one member of the family was asked to phone him and invite him to stay; the family is about to move to a new flat.
- The best man at a wedding has to be told of a sudden change of plan.
- A friend has offered to bring a heavy iron stove in his own truck; A suddenly remembers that the friend does not know exactly where to come, but he hopes that B will have remembered to tell him.
- A difficult young man has asked to join A and B (who had hoped to be alone) on a short trip to Edinburgh; A has promised to take him, but B was supposed to make the contact.

Unit 2.10

- Two young yachtsmen in a home-made boat talking to an experienced sailor before a big race.
- Two men watching their country's representatives in a canoeing contest on TV.
- A professional boat-builder talking to a man who wants to sail the Atlantic single-handed in a hollowed-out log.

- A journalist trying to stop a mad friend from going over the Niagara falls in a plastic ball.
- A father and mother discussing their son's chances in a Trans-Africa motor-bike rally.
- Two prisoners of war discussing the plan of escape suggested to them by a newcomer to the camp.

Unit 2.11
- A 'pushy' businessman wants to make sure his sales representative is invited to an important reception; the man he is speaking to does not wish to let him.
- A is a member of an exclusive club, where a special celebration is to be held; B, who has been invited by A, wishes to bring a friend; A knows the friend and would be embarrassed if he or she came.
- A young girl would very much like to go out with her elder brother, but he thinks she is still too young; she suggests he should pretend she is not his sister, but he does not care for the idea.
- An excursion, for the employees of a factory only, is being organised by B; A would like to bring his ageing mother, whom B knows personally; B tries, politely, to put him off.
- Two children are very excited by the idea of visiting a submarine of which their uncle is commander; they are worried, however, that they might not both be allowed on; their uncle teases them, pretending this is true.

Unit 2.12
- A party of hikers stayed overnight at a small inn; one of the party left by herself earlier in the morning; she cannot be found.
- A spy film, in which two secret agents are waiting for an informer to arrive from a dangerous mission.
- A ceremonial opening (e.g. of a road/a building/swimming-pool) has been held up because the most important guest has not yet arrived; the organiser is getting impatient.
- The police are tracking a woman kidnapper in open fields.
- A safari expedition, that was supposed to be joined by another land-rover, has been held up.

Unit 2.13
- A French friend has called up an English couple; the husband, whose French is not too good, answered the phone; all he remembers clearly is that there was an invitation to lunch.
- One of the typists at a large office took a message for the director during lunch; she clearly did not realise how important the message was.
- Mother has answered the phone for daughter; daughter wants to know far more than mother can tell (e.g. is Gérard coming alone? is he coming by car? etc.).

– Wife has a French cousin, who often drops in without warning; husband answered the phone; he is not very helpful as he hoped to be free at the weekend.

Unit 2.14
– An elderly woman (who insists on dyeing her hair a striking shade of purple), known to her colleagues as a highly moral person, has been seen at a disreputable night club.
– Scene from a Western; the hero is searching for his 'girl'.
– Two neighbours gossiping about a pretty girl from the same street, who has been seen in a strip–tease club.
– A jealous husband talking to a private detective whom he has asked to watch his wife.
– The editor of a gossip column talking to a journalist who claims to have seen a woman politician at a notorious bar.

Unit 2.15
– A messenger is stopped by a porter (at a hotel? a large firm?); he has an urgent telegram to deliver, which must be signed for.
– A painter, who has just finished a portrait of an important politician, is trying to get past the guard at the Ministry.
– An elderly man, carrying a large bouquet of flowers, is stopped, to his embarrassment, by the doorman of the bank where he works . . .
– A young man, coming into a hospital with a large basket of fruit, is stopped by the duty nurse.

Unit 2.16
– Two strangers waiting in a queue outside a public building (to vote? to get unemployment benefits? to donate blood?).
– A traveller, whose ticket is in order and whose luggage has been checked, waiting to get on board a boat; he is an impatient man, and is travelling first–class.
– At the police station; several suspects have been brought in for examination after an assassination attempt; one of these does not understand why he has been arrested.
– Outside a crowded theatre; a woman arrives late, to find her friend standing in a long queue although they already have tickets.
– A small border crossing, where a long line of cars is waiting; a journalist, who has been sent on a special assignment, is anxious to get through.

Unit 2.17
– Two elderly British tourists abroad for the first time, annoyed by a waiter who seems to expect a larger tip.
– Two Australians taking a taxi in London for the first time.
– A foreigner trying to explain to someone from another country why certain service charges had been included in his bill.

- A travel agent assuring two suspicious travellers that their package-tour is truly all-inclusive.
- A member of the staff of a firm is about to leave; a collection has been organised for her; one of the new members of staff did not realise how much it was customary to give.
- A couple have just moved into a small village; they gave some old clothes to a local charity, but the organiser of the charity does not seem to be satisfied.

Unit 2.18

- Two people from different countries, who have recently met; one is asking the other, who is a young doctor, about the scheme for getting young doctors to work in the provinces.
- A father, whose son has just entered the police force/the army/government service, is talking to a senior official about his son's wishes.
- A journalist interviewing a foreign Minister about a programme of 'voluntary' work for juvenile delinquents.
- One young man talking to another about doing his military service.
- A young man talking to his sister, who has recently joined a large petrol company and does not want to be sent to their northern branch.
- Two characters in a play about a totalitarian state.

Unit 2.19

- A young man has a box of dangerous snakes/a pile of smelly washing/a case of excellent wine, which he wants to leave with a friend.
- A boy-friend, by profession a zoologist, has returned from collecting specimens in Africa; he wants to know if the girl's mother would let him leave his baby crocodiles/tropical spiders/lizards/water rats in her flat until he can have them collected by his laboratory.
- A musician with a large double-bass is trying to persuade the left-luggage attendant at a busy London station to look after his instrument.
- At a smart hotel a wealthy-looking guest asks the receptionist if he could leave a human skeleton (he is a surgeon) at the desk . . .
- At a large department store, a lady asks if she can leave her shopping at the enquiries desk . . .

Unit 2.20

- A man in hospital being visited by a 'mate'.
- An inspector talking to the director of a penitentiary about conditions for the inmates.
- A new arrival at a special hospital for the mentally disturbed talking to one of the old patients.
- A son visiting his father in an old folk's home.
- The lady governess of a woman's prison talking to a journalist from a magazine.

Unit 2.21

– A man, who has been working several years for his firm, has asked for special long leave; this has been refused to him though it was granted to a younger colleague.
– A young girl wants to leave her parents and live in a flat by herself; her father will not hear of it.
– A man, whose business is likely to be ruined by the building of a new road, is complaining to an official; he claims that other businessmen are being allowed to apply for special compensation . . .
– A young photographer, who had made photographs of an actress during rehearsal without her permission, had hoped to get more photographs; the actress is not willing . . .
– The eighteen year old son of an ex-professional football player has a scheme to set up his own publishing firm; his father thinks this is a dangerous idea.

Unit 3.1

– An enthusiast of Stockhausen/Wagner/Mahler, etc. playing his whole collection of records to a long-suffering friend.
– A visitor to a country house being shown the *whole* of the garden and grounds.
– A keen amateur photographer trying to get the perfect photograph of a scene, at the end of a long day out.
– Elderly parents being taken out in the car for the day by their son.
– An enthusiastic pianist with a captive audience of two friends.
– A foreign friend being taken around the British Museum.

Unit 3.2

– Someone who has just been to a spiritualist meeting.
– A rather snobbish person who has just been to a pop festival.
– An overweight person who has been dragged along to a yoga class for the first time.
– A teacher of English who has just come out of a meeting where an 'expert' has been expounding his miracle method for learning languages.
– A housewife who has just come back from a session of psycho-drama/'free expression'/etc.

Unit 3.3

– Two East European students invited to an English home where the wife has prepared a 'speciality' from their country which is unrecognisable to them.
– The manager of the local branch of a company awaiting the arrival of his London boss. The only thing he does not like is people who make too much fuss!
– A wife anxious to make a good impression on the brother of her husband, who is coming to stay. The husband is vague and unhelpful.

– An anxious animal lover expecting the arrival of an unusual animal he/she will be looking after for the next few weeks.

Unit 3.4
– A missing antique motor-car has been found.
– An escaped leopard has been sighted by a zoo-keeper.
– The police have come to report to the owner that his stolen picture has been found. The owner put it there himself to cause a sensation.
– A statue was lost the day before it was to have been unveiled. Now the bottom half only has been found.
– One nuclear scientist is talking to another about a box of radioactive material which was lost while on its way from a reactor to a power station.
– Two detectives working on the same case think they have both found a missing safe – but in different places.

Unit 3.5
– A professional photographer with an advertising agent looking for a suitable picture.
– A new secretary who has typed a letter full of mistakes. The second version is a little better, and the boss has not the time to get a third version.
– The owner of a fashion shop reassuring a young designer who has been criticised by another person in the shop.
– A young journalist has been complaining that no one takes any notice of his work. A colleague has taken this up with the editor – who is a busy man.
– An artist who makes counterfeit money feels neglected by those who use him.
– A rheumatic patient being massaged by an eager masseur/masseuse.

Unit 3.6
– A husband, who has been sent out to buy some material to match the curtains, comes back with the wrong shade.
– An artist, showing a bank manager his final design for a mosaic inside the bank.
– An obstinate house-painter, who has painted the kitchen all the wrong colour.
– A child explaining his painting to a logical and unimaginative adult.
– A publicity photographer showing his client a photograph intended to advertise peppermints.
– Two inmates of a mental hospital talking about a painting one of them has done.

Unit 3.7
– The hotel boiler has broken down, so there is no hot water for the guests. The manager has sent an employee to see how the repair man is getting on.

- The manager of an electrical components shop, who has been waiting for a consignment of special transistors.
- Father asking son whether the car will be ready at the garage. He needs it for a weekend trip.
- Husband, sent out by wife to buy curtain material, has forgotten to buy the hooks that go with it.
- A keen fisherman has sent out his son to buy some special fishing tackle; he has come back without the hooks.
- A film producer, waiting for the list of people he has engaged the previous day plus some replacements for unsuitable actors, finds that a mistake has been made at the actors' agency!

Unit 3.8
- A housewife has made elaborate preparations for a dinner for the husband's new boss and wife, who now say they cannot come.
- A couple have invited two other single people to play tennis; one of them has now rung up to say she cannot come.
- Young lovers about to go away on a camping holiday together; the girl has changed her mind.
- A rather boring girl rings up to say she cannot come to a party; the host is secretly rather relieved.
- A girl, who has been invited for the weekend largely because she has a car and the hosts will be able to make use of it, has rung up to say she has had a breakdown.

Unit 3.9
- Parents talking about whether or not to take their son out of a mental hospital.
- Two horse-racing trainers talking about a young horse in training.
- The director of a hospital for training spastic children, and a parent who is taking away his son.
- A couple have been hiding a man wanted by the police; the husband wants to take him to another, safer, hiding-place.
- A probation officer and the director of a remand home talking about whether or not to release a teenager from the remand home.

Unit 3.10
- The organiser of a political meeting is speaking to the manager of a conference centre where he plans to hold a meeting.
- A difficult guest at a party has gone onto the balcony to get away from the rest of the people; the hostess is worried about him.
- A young couple are discussing the plans for their wedding reception on the telephone; he would like to hold it in the garden of his parents' house – she is not so sure.
- A guest at a chalet in the mountains is enquiring about the host's father, who apparently prefers to stay out in the fresh air.

- A student amateur dramatic society is putting on a performance of *A Midsummer Night's Dream* at their college. They want to do it in the open air. The principal of the college is not convinced that this is necessary.

Unit 3.11
- A middle-aged couple who do not normally drink alcohol are being pressed to a drink by a hard-drinking lawyer they have met on holiday.
- Two drug addicts discussing the relative merits of a 'weed' they both smoke.
- A wine connoisseur offering a range of his cellar to a novice.
- A son who has become very wealthy is entertaining his parents, who are not accustomed to his 'life-style'.

Unit 3.12
- An ageing couple have had a breakdown while on holiday in a foreign country. A passing fellow-countryman has picked them up and put them in a hotel in the nearest town and arranged for their car to be repaired the next day.
- A middle-aged couple have had difficulty in ordering a meal in a Hong Kong restaurant. A kind Chinese gentleman has helped them.
- An English couple on holiday have had their luggage stolen from the hotel. The manager has moved heaven and earth to get it back for them.

Unit 3.13
- A young photographic enthusiast has borrowed his friend's expensive camera. Unfortunately, the gadget for focusing seems to have got broken – after he dropped it!
- The office manager has lent a movie film he took in the Seychelles to his secretary to show at a party. She had difficulty getting the beginning of the film into the machine . . .
- A woman tennis-player is returning a hair-drier to the flat-mate of a friend. The nozzle has got burnt somehow, but this is easy to replace . . .

Unit 3.14
- A man who has been a miner since the age of fifteen has been made redundant at forty-five.
- A man who has been working in the same firm in the City for thirty years has been dismissed without any evident reason.
- The managing director of a company in a bad financial state is trying to avoid having to explain to the irate wife of a former employee why he was dismissed.
- A wife tries to comfort her husband, who has just been made redundant from a car factory. She doesn't really believe in her own comforting words.

– A local newspaper has been bought up by a bigger company. One of the conditions of sale was the dismissal of an 'awkward' journalist. His wife wants an explanation.

Unit 3.15

– An electricity bill has been sent which seems to be much too high.
– An office manager has received a letter from a trade-union official asking him to be present at a meeting where cuts in staffing are to be discussed.
– Tenants in a block of flats have written a threatening letter about repainting the woodwork to the agent, who considers he has done more than enough for them.
– The organiser of a local environmental protection society has obtained a large number of signatures on a petition to stop the building of a motorway through a piece of woodland. The building contractor/developer refuses to make any modifications.
– The owner of a flat has given his tenant notice to leave, but with no result. He now plans to keep up the pressure.

Unit 3.16

– Two climbers are lost in the mountains. A relative/friend of one of them is doubtful whether the army will be of much help.
– Two rare pumas have escaped from the zoo. It is nightfall. The zoo director is sceptical of the police superintendent's plans.
– Two speleologists are trapped in a cave. The rope-ladder which they used to get into the cave has fallen down after them.
– The parents of a kidnapped teenager discuss what they should do.
– Two private detectives have been caught by the gang they were pursuing and locked up in a meat refrigeration room.
– An expedition from a polar base-camp has failed to return. It is evening. A friend of one of the missing men questions the director of the expedition.

Unit 3.17

– A husband is talking on the plane to a friend about the depressing effect of their flat on his wife.
– A civil servant in London is discussing the possibility of buying a cottage on the Yorkshire Moors and trying to live a 'back to nature' life.
– A young secretary in London is talking to a much better-off friend about her gloomy flat.
– The young wife of a business executive is talking to her mother about the cramped conditions in their flat in the capital. Her husband needs to be in the capital for professional reasons.
– A young office worker wants to change jobs. A friend offers optimistic advice.

Unit 3.18
– A man selling insurance is trying to get into a wary young woman's flat.
– A junior partner in a firm of solicitors has made a private appointment with his girl-friend in the office. The senior partner is trying to find out what she is doing there.
– Two friends have had a lengthy argument. One of them has now returned to the other's flat much later in the evening.
– A dustman is having a bath at the end of a tiring day. His wife is relaying messages from an unexpected visitor at the door.
– A suspicious character has been hovering in an expensive store for some time. The floor manager tries to discover what he is doing there.

Unit 4.1
– A lover apologising to his mistress in bed early in the morning for making a noise during the night.
– A sarcastic neighbour taking revenge on the couple from upstairs who kept him awake till three in the morning with the noise from their decorating and renovating.
– A shame-faced student in a block of flats who has come to apologise to the tenant below for the noise from his party the night before. He has woken up the wrong person – another student like himself.
– One worker in a hostel could neither sleep nor join in the fun from the previous night because he had to get to the factory early.
– A solicitor in a very expensive block of flats went away with his wife and left his son in charge. The ensuing party left debts of honour to be settled all round. This is just one of the neighbours – a retired colonel – who needs to be pacified.

Unit 4.2
– Two businessmen, one of whom does not need to worry about the feelings of the other because *he* is the one who will agree or not to sign the contract.
– A young man on his first date. He is an hour late and very embarrassed by it. She is very anxious not to make him feel worse.
– A worker with a suspected lung disease has been waiting over an hour to see a Harley Street specialist.
– A trade-union official has been waiting to see the managing director of his firm.
– The boss has promised to give his personal secretary a lift home on Friday afternoon. He is a very busy man.
– An industrial spy from an embassy and a worker in an international computer firm.

Unit 4.3

- The sales representative of an international firm is worried in case he has upset a member of a firm he is visiting which he is anxious to be on good terms with. The manager of the firm is not particularly fond of the person in question.
- A talkative 'friend' has blurted out a personal secret in front of the other person's wife. The husband does *not* want to go on talking about it.
- Boy-friend and girl-friend are quarrelling about what she has called his brother. She is a revolutionary Women's Lib. member, he is a 'bourgeois'.
- Two good friends discuss the 'gaffe' one of them has made at a dinner given by the other. One of the guests was the wife of an alcoholic.
- A junior civil servant has been warned several times that a repetition of his unsatisfactory work will lead to dismissal or transfer. He has committed the sin again. His director has now decided what to do and does not wish to discuss the matter further.

Unit 4.4

- The deputy head of the printing section of an organisation for cultural work abroad has agreed exceptionally to print some posters for an exhibition run by another department section. He is now telling his chief about the tough line he took.
- The organiser of a company dance to raise funds for the victims of an earthquake is talking to the managing director about practical arrangements such as printing the invitation cards. Unexpectedly, the latter is well-disposed.
- A teacher has been asked by the chairman of the parent–teacher association to become secretary. He is now talking to his wife about the reluctance of the chairman to provide necessary help.
- A director has agreed to re-decorate the club-room of a local youth club. He claims he needs wall-paper, and the club secretary has refused. Now he is complaining to his wife.

Unit 4.5

- A girl is telling her disapproving boy-friend about the present of perfume an older man has given her.
- The manager of a firm being courted by a larger rival is not pleased to learn that a junior member of his firm has accepted an expensive tape-recorder from the rival firm.
- At an exhibition of Far-Eastern handicrafts a wife liked a shawl so much that she simply 'picked it up' on the way out. The husband is not pleased and is rather worried.
- After a rather weird party the wife is criticising the husband for taking a substance which might have been a habit-forming drug.
- A young photographic enthusiast has been accompanying his boss on a business trip. He is now telling his wife about the pictures his boss wanted him to take of himself with a girl in a very low night-club.

Unit 4.6

- A blasé drama critic meets a friend in the bar of a theatre where a new play is being put on.
- A cynical art critic meets an innocent friend in an art gallery where some naive painters are exhibiting their work. The innocent friend does not wish to show his ignorance.
- Two friends in the cinema discussing a film.
- A young composer has just finished conducting his first symphony. The girl he brought along to impress is slightly less enthusiastic than he might have hoped.
- A middle-aged couple, caretakers of a block of flats, have been given tickets for a concert of Javanese folk-dancing by one of their tenants. He is very enthusiastic; they do not quite know what to say.
- The curator of a museum has had to send off a guest with one of his subordinates on a trip round the entire museum. He now checks up on the guest's reaction.

Unit 4.7

- An experienced film director is trying not to hurt a young producer's feelings about the film he has just made.
- A young novelist has just come back from taking the manuscript of his book to the publisher's. He is now talking to a friend who works in the field of publishing.
- One radio producer has been prevailed on to press another to produce a script written by the son of the Minister of Foreign Affairs about life in Saudi Arabia. The two producers are good friends.
- A young playwright has written a long play about Australian aborigines. His girl-friend, to whom he has given it to read, is trying not to hurt his extremely sensitive feelings.
- The director of an advertising agency is telling one of the film producers who works for the agency on contract that the film he has proposed will not do.

Unit 4.8

- An enthusiastic tourist talking to his far-from-enthusiastic friend. The friend got to bed at four o'clock this morning.
- A group of Japanese businessmen is being entertained for the day by the Chamber of Commerce of——. The two people in charge of organising the day's events are unenthusiastic.
- A well-known actor is doing a tour around Europe on behalf of the British Council. The local representative has rung up his wife at the hotel on one of the actor's free days to find out what he would like to do.
- A father trying to arouse some enthusiasm in his teenage offspring about the town they are visiting.

Unit 5.1
– A married couple have picked up a hitch-hiker abroad. When they come to the frontier, they explain to the hitch-hiker that they are trying to take several expensive machines (including a camera and a tape-recorder) across the border without declaring them. The hitch-hiker offers to help conceal them.
– A young couple are making a profitable trade in smuggling oriental perfumes. This time, they are carrying a greater quantity than usual. They cannot decide how to get it through the customs.
– A group of young men has discovered a chest full of old coins in a field while camping abroad. They are trying to find a way of getting the money back home.
– A family, whose parents fled from Lithuania during the war leaving all their possessions behind, have returned legally to Lithuania to try to recover five precious family portraits. They have already been warned, however, that works of art may not be taken out of the country . . .

Unit 5.2
– The managing-director of a detergent company is giving his ideas on a programme for promoting a new product.
– Two student leaders discuss how to get publicity for a strike they are organising.
– Two organisers of a local fete and dance discuss publicity arrangements.
– The manager of a small touring circus talking to his local representative in the provinces.

Unit 5.3
– A suspicious factory worker is being asked to sign a hire-purchase agreement by a rather nervous salesman.
– A suspicious businessman about to build a new factory is being asked by a persuasive solicitor to sign permission to start work before all the documents are in order.
– One friend is asking another to witness his passport photograph.
– A do-gooder is trying to collect signatures for a petition. The family is so overcome by his smooth talk that they sign.

Unit 5.4
– An overland expedition to Afghanistan is in preparation. The person approached by the organiser has never driven a minibus before.
– The organiser of an excursion to a football match is 'remembering' his old acquaintances at short notice because he needs a driver for the hired minibus. This one is finding the excuse that he hasn't driven one for years.
– Two hiking enthusiasts have proposed a walking tour of the Scottish Highlands to a city friend who has a car (which would be needed to get them there and back). The friend is not enthusiastic.

- Two sisters are trying to persuade their brother to take them to (and back from) a party which he knows will end late.
- A heavy drinker is trying to persuade a more temperate friend to join him on a pub-crawl through several far-flung villages.

Unit 5.5

- A tourist in a politically extremist state has found a wallet containing a large sum of money. His friend, a native of the country, is anxious that he should not get involved with the police.
- A respectable teacher has been to a disreputable night-club over the weekend. On leaving, he found a gun near his car. His colleague advises him to take it to the police.
- A student has found a valuable painting outside his flat. He knows it is from the local museum and is tempted to keep it. His flat-mate is worried.
- A factory worker has discovered a human hand on his way home from work. His wife wants him to report it, but he is worried because he was taking a short-cut across a military air-field, which is closed to the public.

Unit 5.6

- An art connoisseur is about to buy what he thinks is a Van Gogh. His old friend thinks it would be better to get a second opinion.
- A keen gardener has called in a professional horticulturalist to look at an apple tree that looks a bit sick. He is reluctant to accept his advice.
- A wife is advising her obstinate husband to have an X-ray done on his arm, which is all bruised and apparently sprained after a fall at work.
- An abandoned wife is asking a friend to persuade her husband that he has made a big mistake.
- A dentist is looking at his patient's wisdom tooth which really needs to be extracted.

Unit 5.7

- A young girl is planning to go to a pop festival at a country house. Her elder brother is not entirely in favour.
- Mother does not want her well-brought-up daughter to go on holiday to the 'Club Méditerranée'.
- One secretary to another: one is planning to hitch to Morocco on her own, the other has never been farther than Brighton.
- A young climber wants to take his team up the north face of the Eiger in the depths of winter. An experienced climber is trying to dissuade him.
- A teenage girl wants very badly to go to a dance at a remote hotel. She has now arranged to go with her girl-friend, but her father is still against it.

Unit 5.8

- Wife to husband in a block of council flats. She is tired of being complained to by the neighbours. He likes his TV on loud.

- In an army barracks; the corporal orders the private to turn down his radio.
- In a hotel lounge, a guest trying to read, inquires whether anyone else is paying attention to the TV programme.
- A group of motor-cyclists is in the habit of gathering in front of the house every evening. The father of one of them needs some quiet to do his accounts. Mother supports son.